THE THINGS WE KNOW AND DO NOT SAY

THE FUTURE OF OUR CAREER

Alejandro Sanchez-Buitrago

Copyright © 2023 by Alejandro Sánchez-Buitrago Morales

All rights reserved. No part of this book may be reproduced or used in any manner without written permission of the copyright owner except for the use of quotations in a book review.

FIRST EDITION

ISBNs:
Paperback: 978-1-80227-476-9
eBook: 978-1-80227-477-6

Contents

Biography..v
Acknowledgements..vii
Introduction..ix
Prologue..xi

Chapter 1   Be Consistent................................1
Chapter 2   Mentality....................................8
Chapter 3   Life, Your Life.............................14
Chapter 4   Leading.....................................19
Chapter 5   Experiences.................................24
Chapter 6   The Fear....................................28
Chapter 7   Goals in Life...............................33
Chapter 8   Organization................................36
Chapter 9   Business = Relations........................40
Chapter 10 The Peace...................................43
Chapter 11 Love, Help, Selfishness.....................48
Chapter 12 Loneliness..................................54
Chapter 13 Priorities..................................58
Chapter 14 Whatever it Takes...........................62
Chapter 15 What You Need to Sacrifice..................67
Chapter 16 Spiritual Suicide...........................74
Chapter 17 Health......................................78
Chapter 18 Routines....................................83
Chapter 19 Self-Confidence and Trust...................90
Chapter 20 Retirement.................................106
Chapter 21 Countryside Vs City Life...................111
Chapter 22 The Science of Positivity..................115

Chapter 23	Values.	121
Chapter 24	Expectations.	127
Chapter 25	Top Business Life	132
Chapter 26	The Betrayed	137
Chapter 27	Decision.	144
Chapter 28	"Education vs Ignorance".	149
Chapter 29	Failure	154
Chapter 30	Humility and Happiness	161
Chapter 31	Skills vs Surrounders	166
Chapter 32	Gratitude	171
Chapter 33	Escape	175
Chapter 34	Sport "Circus"	179
Chapter 35	Sports in the Community	183
Chapter 36	Sports and the National Identity	189
Chapter 37	Dreams and Mistakes.	198
Chapter 38	Normality and Simplicity.	202
Chapter 39	Context	206
Chapter 40	Money.	213
Chapter 41	Desire vs Giving Up.	217
Chapter 42	Persistence and Determination.	221
Chapter 43	The Mind	224
Chapter 44	Rumours and Jealousy	229
Chapter 45	Acceptation and Adaptation.	236
Chapter 46	Just Love	240
Chapter 47	Mind vs Heart	244
Chapter 48	Freedom.	248
Chapter 49	Honour, Honestly and Dignity.	254
Chapter 50	A Cruel Heart	262
Chapter 51	Contempt and Hate.	266
Chapter 52	Listen, See and Remain Silent	270

Final Statement 274

Biography

Alejandro Sánchez-Buitrago Morales was born in Madrid, Spain, on 3rd October 1989. He is a Sport Management Executive, coach, teacher, and professor. He holds a Bachelor of Science degree in Sport Sciences from Autonomous University of Madrid, a Master of Business Administration (MBA) in Sport Management degree from Europea University of Madrid, a Master of Science in Physical Training and Rehabilitation Therapy in Football degree from the Catholic University of Murcia and a Master's degree in Education from the Camilo José Cela University of Madrid. He also possesses a Professional Licence in Coaching Football and professional certificates related to Strategic Management from The Wharton School of the University of Pennsylvania and in Education from Harvard University.

He has experience in sports management and coaching at several of the best football clubs in the world, including Club Atlético de Madrid, Real Madrid CF and Arsenal FC where he is working at the moment. He is currently the Vice President of the London Football Association, having previously collaborated with Associations such as the Chinese Football Association and the Azerbaijan Football

Association, and having developed projects and consultancies across the five continents.

He has been a lecturer in many fields, including at master's level, through UEFA coaching courses, clinics, research seminars and consultancies. He has also worked as a mentor/tutor and provided consultancy to academic journals and digital TV programmes and has worked as a teacher for both the English and Spanish Departments of Education.

Acknowledgements

I just want to begin this book by saying that I am not a professional writer or a famous person; nor am I the smartest person in the world, but I have lived an intense life, working in a tough business, around the world. Now, here in London, I want to share with whoever wants to read this "book", some of my feelings, thoughts, advice, and even jokes that I think about life. I also have friends who will provide expert advice on many matters. If I know something about life, it is that an honest person like me will never have many friends, but the ones who are my true friends will be real, honest, and super-professional ones, and those are the most important traits for me.

Maybe you will not like everything that you will read, and perhaps I will be wrong in some of my advice but don't judge me, because I am not perfect, but you need to know that what you will read is coming from the real world. I am just trying to be happy inside my own world, and I want to show you what I have learnt and what I will learn in the next few years because I don't know anything yet.

This book is dedicated to my parents, Gregorio Sánchez-Buitrago and Aurora Morales. I respect you, I care about you, and I love you, forever and ever.

"Oír, ver y callar"
"Listen, see and remain silent"

Introduction

This book focuses on the improvement of the personal and professional life of each person, a word that defines a way to organize and carry out the processes that we do day by day in our life.

We must understand life as a single whole, where the "contexts" are the key to improving our life and our whole management of it. Life is a mix of feelings and experiences; life is cruel and tough but full of chances and opportunities. This book shows both the positives and negatives of life but leaves a door open for better things based on my experience.

This book is divided into chapters where we talk about human contexts, and where we try to deliver a vision and advice about how to deal with them. In other chapters, we focus on providing examples and consultancy about how to improve as a professional.

The writing will be simple and easy to understand. You will get the author's opinions, advice, and vision, and, at the end of each chapter, expert personal advice from many people. The experts' advice will come from personal friends of the author, who have achieved top goals in their personal and professional lives. In other chapters, you will find quotes with an important message that will make us reflect. All of them will provide a direct message to help the reader because all of them had enough experience to be able to provide good feedback about all the stuff that we try to analyse and talk about in the book.

When we are seventeen, we need to make an important decision about what we want to be or do for the rest of our life. This book is focused on helping young people to find their way, to open the eyes and the mind and to be able to decide the way they want to go forward with more foundation and knowledge. We also focus on young footballers, because they need advice on how to deal with all the contexts that they have experienced since they came into that business.

Life is easy and difficult at the same time. We cannot choose what's going to happen, e.g., where we are born, but we can choose the path that we want to take to fight for our dreams. This book can provide some help for that young person who thinks that everything is very easy and we can trust in everything and everybody; because life is not that and they need to know it. We want them to be able to plan, be organised and be independent young adults.

That's why I have written this book at the age of 32 because I am still young enough to understand and remember what young people feel, but I have been in the world for a while, working around the world in different businesses, so I can give them some advice about it. Also, the experts who have helped in this book are all older and more experienced people so we need to read and feel what they want to tell us. We will also have quotes, to make the reader "think" and look introspectively.

To sum up, I really think that this book will help somebody, just as it has already helped me a lot to be able to share thoughts and ideas with myself and with the people who helped with their advice. We may not be good enough as individuals but we are stronger and better as a team and we need to get the best from the people around. This is the message my book focuses on, so enjoy it!

Prologue

Abián Perdomo Alonso

Real Madrid CF Director of Training Methodology and Education. First Team Assistant Coach. Master and Author. UEFA Champions League and La Liga winner season 2021/22.

One of our targets in life consists of the tireless search for happiness, this tendency being directed, on most occasions, towards ourselves, and on other occasions towards others. For example, many times we consider that our main objective in life consists of being happy and making others happy, but perhaps in the search for that happiness we are losing the true happiness, which is on the way... not at the finish line... but on the way to getting that target...

Happiness is one of the main objectives of the human being, that is, of an individual of indivisible unity, of a rational mind, who speaks, feels, works, creates, develops... We are species, evolution, thoughts, feelings, we are the way, and we are part of those "roots" that are part of our life.

Throughout our life, we travel different paths, where the origin of each of them starts from our identity and our natural tendency, which guides us at the beginning, in the direction of our "walks" and in those life goals that we are considering.

Therefore, one of our main life objectives should be to know who we are and recognize ourselves in each of the interaction processes that we generate in our day-to-day lives and to know ourselves in each context in which we interact. Thus, we will be able to act in a more adjusted and balanced way.

The individual grows in a society that he/she transforms day by day and, at the same time, this society transforms the individual. This human being is the fruit of the anchors of the past and the illusions of the future, not often focusing his/her vision on the present. The objectives must be set in the long, medium, and short term, but the focus must be placed on the short and the medium, to be able to project into the long term. That does not mean that we do not look at the long term, because we always have to look far, but to get there, many times, "you have to generate advantages nearby." However, along the way, our fears can always reappear, often coming from our past emotions, and that sometimes blocks us in the achievement of our goals, which is why we must always be aware of emotions, no matter what they are, and figure out how to manage them.

Dear reader, I am not really someone to give advice, but simply, from these paragraphs, I have tried to contribute my degree of "immaturity" in the matter and, in my humble opinion, I can only tell you this - never stop knowing who you are and where you came from; become aware of you and the things that surround you, and remember your roots when deciding what you want and where you are going. Never stop walking and build your own path in life based on what makes you feel happy regarding your goals and needs. Always see the happiness that is in your daily life and that your place of happiness doesn't conflict with others.

Writing is complex, venturing to write is even more difficult and exposing your ideas to others, or what you are, feel or think is not only complex but also requires courage, since writing is exposing yourself to being judged. That is why I invite you to judge each of my paragraphs and that from this judgment, you may reflect on my thoughts, because my contribution in this text does not pretend to teach or establish a doctrine about something, but to start a pleasant path of reflection by your side.

Therefore, in the same way, I ask you, on what path do those human beings who develop a sporting activity walk? What do we think of them? How and why do we value them? Do we analyse, evaluate, or judge them? Also, the most important question - what do we intend with everyone with whom we interact, deal and/or value?

Through these questions, I have tried to introduce this great work to develop not only a great professional of high value, but also a friend with whom to walk in these beautiful processes of reflection. Years ago, I had the opportunity to meet a magnificent person, radiant with energy and with a great capacity for adaptation and evolution in each context through which he passed. Alejandro is work, dedication, and passion, which he shows in each of the chapters in this book.

Thanks, Alejandro, for exposing yourself, thanks for teaching us your ideas, thanks for venturing into this dangerous attempt to "dominate the waves of the sea", to try to control the uncontrollable to guide us on the way, yet always with respect for that power of nature. Thank you for counting on me to contribute my little grain of reflection and invite the reader to navigate this book, generating a process of constant reflection.

Everyone asks about the key to success; I do not have it, I do not know it and I doubt that I will ever have it or know it, but from my experience and through my reflection processes, I can only say to each of the readers of this book that in each activity that you develop, you dare to express your talent without fear, that you put all your effort and heart into it, not to compete or overcome another person, even if you consider them as a direct opponent, but you must do it as a process of personal improvement because every day, we compete against ourselves. In addition, try to accept each of the movements of your life with courage and be willing to lose, because defeat is not to be feared and winning is being brave, since both in life and in sport, you will combine victories with defeats.

Dear reader, whatever the cost, pursue your dreams and help to achieve the dreams of others. Having a path or a goal offers us a direction. The objective in the journey of the path may change, it may be variable and dependent on various factors, but we must set ourselves life goals that provide us, that feed our happiness and our hearts because remember that everything depends on being happy in the here and now and we must find happiness in the daily meaning of our life.

Congratulations, Alejandro, for this great work, congratulations on your courage, walking without fear, walking in search of your goals regardless of the stone that presents on the path, and many congratulations for sharing knowledge, experience, and reflection.

Talking about football is talking about life; talking about life is talking about human beings who interact in society and talking about human beings who interact in this society is talking about common and opposite goals, emotions, and paths, full of experiences, that seek happiness, therefore, everything revolves around talking about life…

To conclude, I consider that many times, we focus on achieving our own objectives and not on helping others to achieve theirs, looking at the two paths as different, but I want to link this end with my beginning and that is why I ask you this: To help myself and others, the first thing I do is ask myself who I am and who we are. What do I do in the place where I am and why? What do I want and what do others need from me? And above all, what degree of assessment do I make of myself? May each of you have enough personality to offer your own answers to these questions. I conclude with the belief that tells me that we always ignore our "ego" and perhaps many of us think that it is not part of us. However, this writer considers that, at best, we must not allow the ego to limit us.

Prologue

Dear friend Alejandro and dear readers, I want you to always remember that we are where we are and that we will always see each other in a beautiful space that I call "the green" (the pitch), that space in which all of us, both children and adults, have shared a wide range of objectives, projects, and illusions.

I propose that you always remember that we see what we know or what we think we know and that our gaze may be conditioned by who we are, therefore, we do not often see what happens because our thoughts and emotions cloud or condition that look. Never forget that from everything to nothing and from nothing to everything, there is less than one step; that is, there is less than one step that can relocate or misplace us in our daily walk, so be aware of everything and learn to give them the value and relevance they have.

Ultimately, you must live, be happy, let everybody live and make others happy.

CHAPTER 1

Be Consistent

Being consistent is hard in life because a lot of things happen to us that make us have ups and downs. We just need to be very focused on a goal and to keep the mind clear to never lose that focus, that thing that makes us be consistent and deliver effort. It is a mix of knowing who you are, what you want and what you must do, and of course, we need to do it every day.

But where do we get this energy when we feel down?

There are brilliant people who have the skill to know what they want and pursue it no matter what happens, but they do not get to that level of effort when they feel lost or down. This leads us to think that being consistent is something that comes from the "mind", and it is true because, in the end, everything starts and ends in the mind. We can go for a run if we are not physically well or need to relieve ourselves of stress, but the mind is more difficult to satisfy.

There is nothing else; it is all or nothing. If your mind works, everything is possible; if it does not work, give up or ask for help because you will never be able to give your 100% and you will not be happy with it. Here comes another key - happiness - because everything is connected. We make more effort when we believe in what we are doing and that makes us enjoy it and makes us feel happy. We need to control our emotions because if not, they can work against us.

Have you ever wanted to do something but were not motivated to achieve it? So, even though you wanted to, you couldn't; it's like walking in quicksand. It is the same sensation that we feel when we do not have confidence in ourselves; we are not connected with the goal, and we need that mental connection.

Therefore, we talk about something strictly mental, something that comes from the inside, but also something that comes from an outlined plan, a plan thought out, directed, and elaborated on that makes us feel "safe" and confident; makes us feel connected with what we do, and we can work to improve it.

So, could we plan our consistency, our happiness? Could we work to create our own consistency?

The answer is yes because we can create our own world where we can be happy. We can take control of our life, improve in self-confidence, know ourselves more, know how we treat ourselves and from there, have a life plan aimed towards the goal. People say that when you smile, even if you are not happy, you relax the mind, and it feels better. This is how the mind works and we must control what we feel and think and be balanced with ourselves and the context to be able to pursue what we want.

Now, once we are clear about what we want, we go for it.

How you do things, is important too. To do things with honour and dignity is a basic pillar in life. It is not necessary to "sell" anyone to achieve your goals, and if that goal requires doing that, it may not be the correct goal. Of course, you must be smart and know how to "play", but you should never lose your principles because otherwise, you will become the same as those people you criticize. Yet, it is no less true that these days, words like honour and dignity have almost been forgotten; there is still some honour, and we can find it in some people, but in general, in the world where we live today, it's been lost. We have lost some of the values, but if some humanity remains in us, we must be "consistent" and follow this path.

Be Consistent

To be consistent implies a moral conviction, not only at the social level but in your own being. I am talking here of the purest goodness, which is being able to be good or bad and choosing to be good. Being good to impress others or because you don't know how to be bad, is not true goodness; that comes when someone has the option to be good or bad and chooses to be good.

If the world is losing this true goodness, it is because the education that children are receiving in school and at home is not adequate or it's just because we have lost the values definitively. It's my own belief that both of these contribute to the situation and we really need to change it, or we will lose the values that our ancestors created for us.

Children don't have good reference points or role models, not at school, and not at home because the parents are working and they cannot educate their children. Even if we look at the TV shows, it's embarrassing to see what kind of people succeed there. Even if you try to care about something or change it, you will be called a "fool"; so, the question is, why do we have to care about it if it's all lost? Well, sometimes I believe it's a lost cause but it's our responsibility to die fighting for the good and to at least try to educate our children, or the people that we have around, in a good way. Most just want us to be ignorant and to control our minds, but we have a chance to lead our life, and it all depends on us.

Being consistent begins in the mind and finishes in our heart, so organise your mind and never lose your heart; you will "walk" on the right path to your goals.

Extra comment/thought/feeling:
Gregorio Sánchez-Buitrago
Engineer and Economist. Former Business Director and Consultant.

The Things We Know and Do Not Say

(Spanish-English)
La CONSISTENCIA para alcanzar OBJETIVOS. Introducción.

Consistencia	Sinónimos	Antónimos	Consistir
	Compacto	Inconsistente	Componerse
	Duro		Constar
	Sólido		Recluirse
	COHERENTE		Estribar
	FIRME		Radicar
			Residir
			Gravitar
			BASARSE
			APOYARSE

Resumen de conceptos relacionados; APOYO EN BASE FIRME Y COHERENTE

CONSISTENCY to achieve OBJECTIVES. Introduction.

Consistency	Synonyms	Antonyms	Consist
	Compact	Inconsistent	Compose
	Hard		Record
	Solid		Withdraw
	COHERENT		Stirrup
	FIRM		File
			Reside
			Gravitate
			Be based
			Support

Be Consistent

Summary of related concepts; SUPPORT ON A FIRM AND COHERENT BASIS

Objetivo	Sinónimos	Antónimos	Objeto
	Estado de ánimo		Cosa
	Finalidad		Elemento
	Propósito		ENTE DIFERENCIADO
	META		
	ASPIRACIÓN		
	IDEAL		

Resumen de conceptos relacionados;

PRIMACIA DEL OBJETO FRENTE AL SUJETO

INDEPENDENCIA DE VALORES MORALES DEL OBJETO FRENTE A OPINIÓN DE INDIVIDUOS

RELATIVO A OBJETO EN SÍ, NO A NUESTRO MODO DE PENSAR/SENTIR

Objective	Synonyms	Antonyms	Object
	Mood		Thing
	Target		Element
	Meaning		DIFFERENTIATED ENTITY
	GOAL		
	ASPIRATION		
	IDEAL		

Summary of related concepts.

PRIMACY OF THE OBJECT VERSUS THE SUBJECT

INDEPENDENCE OF MORAL VALUES OF THE OBJECT AGAINST THE OPINION OF INDIVIDUALS

RELATED TO THE OBJECT ITSELF, NOT TO OUR THINKING/FEELING MODE

La consistencia para alcanzar objetivos. - *ACTITUD Y FIRMEZA MORALES SEGUIDA DE ACTUACIÓN FIRME, PARA ALCANZAR EL OBJETIVO DESEADO, QUE DEBE SER COHERENTE CONTIGO, INDEPENDIENTE DE TI, PERO COHERENTE CON TUS VALORES MAS PERSONALES.*

Consistency to achieve objectives. - MORAL ATTITUDE AND FIRMNESS FOLLOWED BY FIRM ACTION, TO ACHIEVE THE DESIRED OBJECTIVE, WHICH MUST BE CONSISTENT WITH YOU, INDEPENDENT OF YOU, BUT CONSISTENT WITH YOUR MOST PERSONAL VALUES.

Consistency requires will and attitude over time and this is only possible if you believe in what you are trying to achieve.

To promote consistency, it must be planned as much as possible, prioritizing the means and actions necessary to achieve the objective before acting.

If possible, try to subdivide the final objective into partial objectives. In this way, motivation is maintained over time and the discouragement of seeing it as unattainable is avoided.

The main plan must be drawn up to achieve the objective, without prejudice to having a plan B in case the main one fails.

To believe in the long term in what you want to achieve, the objective, this must be independent of you and your immediate desires, and at the same time, it must be consistent with your basic values because otherwise, it would not be worth the effort.

The objective must be possible to achieve, even though it is extremely difficult, otherwise, over time, one may grow increasingly discouraged.

If the objective is achieved, this should not be the end of everything; it should be the beginning of a new objective, because if not, what is life? If you fail, you must be prepared for the frustration that will occur, question why you failed and think that the important thing was that you tried.

Bibliography

Nuevo Espasa Ilustrado. (2000). Diccionario Enciclopédico. / New Espasa Ilustrate. (2000). Encyclopedic.

Diccionario de sinónimos y antónimos. (2004). Santillana. / Dictionary of synonyms and antonyms. (2004). Santillana.

CHAPTER 2

Mentality

Sometimes, when you think you are in a bad moment or situation, something worse comes along that makes you see that in life, we can always be worse. It is in those moments when you must show what kind of mentality you have. The key is how you manage your own feelings, how positive you are and despite any situation, how much you want to improve in life and go forward. Try to be flexible about what happens, not to settle, but to adapt, as that is the keyword of life. There's nothing more than that.

"Adapting" to the context is the key because, in life, things happen day by day, good and bad, and we must continue whatever happens. We must adapt to what happens and continue to live and fight for the life we want. Everything is a matter of how you assimilate things, how you face problems and trust in yourself and your organizational capacity.

Somebody said once that "Life is ten percent what happens to you and ninety percent how you respond to it". But nothing is easy; you must believe in yourself and be there, because the improvement comes every day, in every step you take, in every second and detail, in every inch you go. But how problems make you feel, how you can face them, that feeling is the key to being able to solve them in a good way or sometimes not solve them at all.

We must be aware that every single day, we have chances to change our future; it is up to us to fight for it or not. We don't have bad luck forever; you must work hard to have good luck. You create your own luck, so it depends on you what you want to do; It just depends on whether you really want it or not. Winners always want to; losers use any excuse to quit.

Our mentality is key to how we see the world and we adapt to the things that happen in it, and for that, the key is to feel good about ourselves and try harder next day, because every day we have a new chance. We just need to take a seat and write down what we want, and from there, plan the best way to get it. Life is easier than we all think - to know yourself and what you want is just the first step; from there, everything is possible. Every day is a new day, and something good can happen, so one hundred percent, being positive is the key; being negative increases your bad luck and does not help anyone except your enemies.

The only person who can think that you cannot achieve something is simply yourself. What others think does not matter; the only things that matter are what you think. The first reaction to the problem is the key to being able to solve it or not. You must relativize things; everything has a solution - ALWAYS. We must have a positive reaction and patience, and from there, you can plan to achieve your goal; it's as easy as that.

A big mistake that we all have is to let people influence us in our own decisions, our own dreams, and goals, just because we are social animals and we "need" to feel respect from others. We've got that inside us, but it's down to us to change it and try to live our own life with our own mistakes and good moments. If you do something just because someone says you should, that means that the rest of the people should follow what a group of people say; find your path and be happy with it and yourself.

People will tell you that it is impossible to achieve something just because they are unable to achieve it. Listen to people who love you but never heed comments from negative people with complexes and fears.

ADAPTABILITY + CONFIDENCE + WILLINGNESS + PATIENCE

Having a good mentality only depends on one person - on you. The rest will be excuses that people make for not accepting their own mistakes. If you have fears, you must know how to face them and find a way to improve. Everything has a solution in life, except death. In football, it will not be easy to always maintain a positive mentality, but we must lean on ourselves, our family, and our teammates. We should let others give us love and help us because many times, the problem is that we want to do everything alone and not accept help. We must be brave to open our hearts and minds, let good and bad things come, and solve problems with positivity, with the belief in our ability as an unshakable weapon. Life is two days, and we use one of them to sleep, so be positive because, with the right attitude, everything has a solution.

Extra comment/thought/feeling:
Gabriel Hernández Paz
Former professional water polo player. Two times World Champion and named best player of the championship. Olympics as a player and coach for the Spanish National Team. LEN Champions League winner. Businessman and entrepreneur.

Reaching the elite of a sport like football is something extraordinary. Millions of children play around the world dreaming of the possibility of making that dream come true. The one who gets it is a lucky person, a very lucky person, a super lucky person! Being able to earn a living doing what you like the most and in a sport like football in which there is no economic limit, is clearly a goal only available to the privileged, and for that, we have to be thankful every day.

It is clear that to get there, you have to sacrifice, and sometimes, pay a very high price, surely giving up very important things along the

Mentality

way such as friends, family, etc. ... but always keeping in mind that the reward is much higher than any sacrifice made since although everything that costs is true, we must think that millions of children around the world sacrifice themselves in the same way that we do and yet they do not arrive, and we must remember this every day during our entire sports career and thank destiny (in addition to our work and sacrifice) for the opportunity that life offers us. Being grateful is very important and I think that having the ability to value and be grateful for what we have achieved has to inspire us and give us feedback daily to continue working and also help us to rise up in difficult moments. These moments will surely come and must be mastered by remembering how difficult it was to get there, how lucky we are to earn a living making our passion our profession, and how proud we make those who see us, all those who have crossed into our lives and shared time and experiences with us before becoming professional players.

The professional world mainly requires having a personality. Personality is and will be a great asset of any athlete and of any person in general, and, from the first moment, it must be nurtured. Entering a professional locker room requires you, above all, to have a strong and marked personality. Personality is mainly beyond quality or talent, what a coach and teammates long for, or what high competition demands. Personality is seriousness at work, sacrifice, an example of solidarity, positivity even in the most difficult moments (no one wants to be near a negative or pessimistic person), self-demanding and demanding of your colleagues, continuously searching for our limits to improve and get out of our comfort zone. It is also helping colleagues in everything and being generous with compliments to your teammates, no matter how small the detail may be. This praise is highly valued by any human being, the simple fact of receiving recognition for our actions no matter how small... 'thanks for the pass', 'thanks for closing the counterattack when I lost the ball ...'). Do not be influenced by anyone; be you, always you, and never do what others want or let yourself be carried away by anyone. If not, and you betray yourself, you will regret it. The world is full of seductive and manipulative people, and you have to realize who is seductive or manipulative around you ... never listen to them, be strong and go your way. If you stop being yourself for a little while, you could destroy your sports career, so show your personality and always do only what you really want to do.

Upon reaching the professional world, you will hear the word leader or leadership. In my opinion, there are many types of leaders, and we could say that a leader is not only the friendliest or the most charismatic of the team, or the one who has the most capacity to transmit or seduce the group. For me, a strong team must be made up of many leaders beyond their intrinsic personality capabilities. A leader is any player who is an example for his/her teammates. A partner who works and sacrifices himself/herself, who is close and affectionate, who helps everyone, who is altruistic in the field and brave, very brave, without fear ... that is a leader, an example for all. If you do not have all these virtues, practise them and you will improve. If you are shy and do not dare, or it is difficult for you to be affectionate, remember that we are all shy, but that cannot prevent you from developing one of the most important things - communication. When you get to the locker room, communicate, ask, be interested, and be grateful. You will earn the respect of the veteran player because he/she will see that you show interest, and he/she will see that you are involved, and he/she will be surprised if you are able to flatter him/her without kissing his/her arse.

The last thing I would like to say is that you must enjoy every day to the fullest; you must feel what you do and do it with all your passion, every day, without exception.

Mentality

You are your own brand, so do whatever you want but always think about what you want people to think when they hear your name, or what you want a colleague to think when they think of you. From there, do whatever you want accordingly.

Enjoy it!!!!

CHAPTER 3

Life, Your Life

Life, your life, is it really yours?

We always have thoughts about life, which is normal because, despite our beliefs, no one knows for sure where we come from and where we are going or what will happen after death. It is a dangerous land of thoughts because we cannot know it and it can destroy us if we spend too much time dwelling on it. Do we really control our lives or are we socially conditioned towards thoughts, a way of living influenced by context from the people who control opinion through the media, etc.?

It is not good to listen to such thoughts too much, because you will never find an answer. Knowing that they want to influence us can help us to become more aware and try to have a more independent life, striving to achieve greater autonomy from our character and personality.

I do not know much more about life than you, reader, but I am sure that everything I think and that forms my character does not come from myself. The experiences around influence your thoughts and how you think and behave in your life. Therefore, in accepting all these facts, you have to try to be "you"; you have to try to live your life without letting it be conditioned too much by the outside. Is it easy? No, it is simply impossible, but once you are aware of it, you can begin to live a real life or at least be aware of more things that happen around you.

Life, Your Life

Does life belong to us, our life?

We all want answers about the topics we have talked about before, but your life will never belong to you until you have the courage to be independent, and that requires reading, analysing, and thinking about what happens to us in the world. Even by that stage, we are still on the starting line because everything is difficult; life is conditioned by us, as well as by the context in which we live.

Do we want to be aware of these things or are we happy living as we live? Maybe we live better in ignorance than not.

I guess nobody wants to be ignorant at first, however, when you have lived a lot, sometimes you would like to ignore many things. It is true and it must be said that the more you know the more you suffer; this is a very great truth. To be aware of the good and bad things in life is dangerous because they can make you feel pain for many things, so, to improve as humans, we must be strong, face up to them and don't give up.

We talked about how we are a mixture of experiences, contexts and our own feelings and thoughts. We agreed that our context affects the way we live, act and feel; so, is it possible to control your life? Well, we can try to control it for a little while; it depends on us, on how many things we expect from others and on our boundaries in certain situations.

The real situation today is that our opinion is not based on our own rational thoughts. It is all manipulated; public opinion is not the result of the reflective thinking of people. Everything is determined by the interest of a few, and they always manipulate the "sheep" as they want. For every one person who reads and thinks, there are a million who only listen and obey.

Where does the problem of how we are come from?

Firstly, because we are not educated to think or analyse, there is no critical thinking. People do not analyse or criticise things based on logical fundamentals. Education curriculums are not programmed to teach young people how to use their minds or how to analyse and criticise what's happening around them. The curriculums are designed just for teaching the basics and to control young people for a while until they are allowed to work. Governments do not care anymore about having smart citizens. They want to divide us into classes, to have enough people for good and bad jobs and also to control us better, because if you are not well educated, you cannot understand what's happening in the country, so you cannot complain about anything.

Secondly, the power, which is economic power, dominates the media and people judge what they see on TV and what they read in the newspapers; so, we're manipulated. We are not educated to think so we do not ask ourselves about anything; they control us, they do not educate us, but they manipulate us. Opinion is manipulated and therefore, so too is happiness. They teach us to think about what we must like, what we must fight for, even the hobbies we must have, for which we live in a false sense of happiness created by others for us. The problem that we have is huge, but anybody can see it, so being aware of it gives us the possibility to change and build our own world. So, don't let other people or the world manipulate your thoughts, feelings, and ideas; try to use critical thinking and build your real happiness.

Taking control of your life depends on three attributes - personality, patience and being organized. Personality is key because you have to know yourself first before others and trust in your thoughts and beliefs and have the control of your emotions to face critical moments. You must also be aware that mistakes are part of future success because the experiences just make you stronger.

We need patience because we live in a big world with many people around, and with many rules and laws and sometimes you need to be aware of this and be calm, even in situations That you don't understand.

Be organized because it is the first step to success. Be organized in your actions and in your thoughts; plan your steps and live a proper life where you take care of yourself first.

Some guidelines to help yourself:

"The most organized person is the laziest one because when you plan your stuff, you don't need to work or think about it again, you just follow the plan."

-The one who is organized in the long run, works much less than the one who is not. Building your own routine and timetable will help you to be more consistent, so be aware of what you need to do every day. It is important to have a balance, living a flexible life, where you have time for yourself along with contact with friends and date time. If you fill your life with organization and have a plan, you will have everything under control, and you will not waste time.

"Think bad and you will be right."

-Be positive but analyse how things could end in a bad way. This way of thinking will prevent you from encountering bad people and the wrong situations that could happen. 'Think bad' is just an action where you control the situation and protect yourself from other mistakes or bad contexts by already having Plan B, and possibly Plan C in place.

"If you go with the wrong people, you will become like them sooner or later."

-Surround yourself with good people and, if it is possible, those smarter than you, as you will always improve with them. If you follow the wrong people, you will finish like them, because we do what we see, even when we don't want to.

"Don't leave till tomorrow the things you can take care of today."

-Everything that you can fix now, do it and don't leave it for tomorrow. Be consistent and an active person, since being lazy and procrastinating will not help you with anything.

"You only own what you don't say."

-Listen, see and be quiet. Your thoughts are yours but only if you don't tell anybody, so talk about them with your real friends and family, but never tell everybody, because there are a lot of people that will use them against you.

"Sit at the door of your house long enough and you will see the corpse of your enemy pass by."

-Being patient will lead you to have better thoughts, and to make decisions based on real ideas and true thoughts. Be patient and wait, because if you keep working, everything will come sooner or later.

"Listening to the right people will lead you to get great things."

-Don't talk; listen to the experienced people; their thoughts will lead you to get great things. The people that talk a lot are the ones that don't have any idea; just listen and build your own life.

"You will never love another person truly if you don't love yourself first."

-Love yourself to be able to love others. It is impossible to love others truly if you don't love yourself properly, as it is impossible to teach someone to be tidy if you are not. Love is the first step to building your own world.

Building your own happiness is based on having control of your life and your feelings, being aware of who you are, what you would like to do and what your targets are. There are many questions to ask yourself but when you have all the answers, you must simply be brave and build your own perfect life.

Life comes with good and bad things, but we will have the opportunity to change it as we like, with personality, patience and being organized.

Extra comment/thought/feeling:
We must understand within each one of us, that everything depends on "us". It all depends on what "you" want to do or what you don't want to do.

CHAPTER 4

Leading

Leading begins with what you think and feel for yourself. We talk about respect, personality, and clear thoughts, but leading is not a term with a unique definition. However, good development of this discipline implies daily perfection, like an athlete or any professional. Leading requires having things very clear within yourself and having the ability to convince others of what you believe. This requires having a great personality and personal confidence.

When I lead, I am moving people's thoughts, messages, ideas, and wishes. It's a way of living, but how to know if it is right or not is the key to improving as a leader.

What makes me a good leader or not?

Life is neither white nor black; it's grey, and it depends on contexts, so, common sense is the key to getting almost everything. Your common sense comes from the experience that you have had in your life - things you have lived, or have learned - so this is the first step. If I want to lead and deliver advice to others, I need to have my mind clear first.

The keys to leadership are based on several pillars, such as self-confidence, respect, and the ability to convince people with your message. Confidence in yourself is key, as we will see in one of the chapters of the book. Even being wrong in ideas, a person with strong self-confidence can achieve great things, because we talk about attitude. The attitude and the energy that you deliver are projected into what you do every day. People follow people with an attitude because they emit good feelings in a world full of fears and lies.

People will follow you if you give yourself respect, and respect is achieved with "deeds" rather than words, although a good use of the word always helps. What you do and how you do it will make people look at you well or badly; these are all sensations, but it is vital to be able to lead without the doubts of people.

Convincing others of what you think and believe is a difficult task. You must get to the depths of the person and their feelings to make others see what you want them to see. It requires experience, handling skills and a deep understanding of the human being.

Leading means being responsible for people, being responsible for their thoughts and their own integrity. You must be clear about who you are and, from there, you have to be clear about your values. Leading is not something individual because to be able to lead, we need to "sell" trust; we need to be trusted by them. We are talking about motivation, and when a group get it, this is stronger than anything.

To lead is to always know what you can do and what you are willing to do for that idea. You don't have to bury yourself for an idea, but you must do it for the people who follow you.

To be a leader, we need to be clear about what we want and how we want to get it, and, from there, motivate others in our thoughts to achieve the goal.

Find the path to building your own destiny, as there is no better guide than ourselves to lead us to the next level. If you believe in this, even if there are people who interfere and want to stop you, you will see it as a chance to improve, even as something that had to happen to reach that final "target".

Leading, therefore, depends on the leader but he/she depends on the group. The union of these is the foundation for the leader to offer his/her skills, and to be able to move and motivate the project to go for the goals.

We need the idea to have strength, and then know how to focus it and take it on the right path. Everything must have a why; nothing should be done for nothing, and the "how" is very important, because you must justify the way things are done to the group. In addition, the attitude you use in the process is essential. The leader must transmit, must make his/her people "feel" what he/she feels to go in the right direction and towards the correct "target".

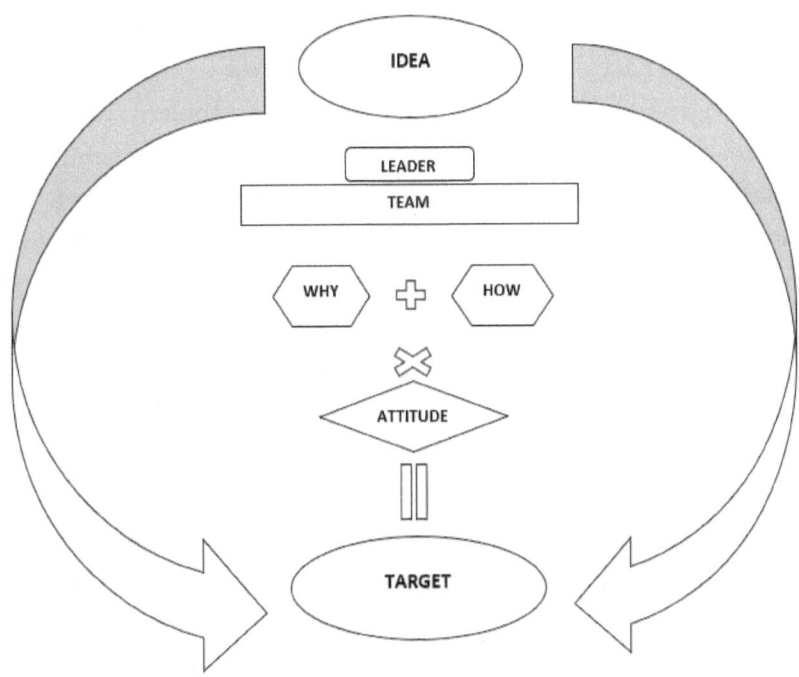

Leadership requires knowledge, experience, empathy, and trust. There may be many more requirements too as we talk about gaining the trust of the people who you need to lead. You must reach their minds and their hearts.

It is said that some are born to lead while others are not. I think you can train to lead and it's been proven. You just need to know how. We have all seen top leaders in different fields like industry, sciences, or sport; there are also differences between them. Some of them have more patience than others, others lead with fear etc. It's so important to lead by example and if you talk about standards, you must be working within those standards as well, which is hard, but being a leader is a tough role.

The most important thing about leading is to lead by example, through hard work, but also you need to make the people believe in what you say. You need to get to that part of the mind but, most importantly, that part of the heart, to let the people believe in you. You need to have experience and prove it, show to everybody that you have lived and learnt; that's what makes people respect you. Moreover, you need to have qualities as a leader, such as being able to talk in public, showing confidence in yourself when you are facing problems, having the capacity to solve issues, and having the patience and experience of somebody that knows how to deal with problems.

It is my honest belief that you either have confidence or not because of the context of your life and the experiences you have had and that makes you confident with yourself. From there, the way to socialize and the ability to convince people have an impact as well. Convincing requires knowledge of the subject and being able to teach it, in addition to adding the life experiences you have had; this will be the greatest weapon for reaching the feelings and the hearts of people, as real experiences always reinforce the message we give.

Leading also requires knowing what we do wrong and sometimes showing that you are like everyone else, without reaching the point where they may think that you are not fit to take control or you are weak.

Leading involves knowing more and controlling everything else, as this will be what makes you trusted. One always looks oneself in the face before others, as the opinion we have of ourselves is key. The motivation, the passion, and what you know about yourself give you all the power that you need. Having confidence in yourself is the key to being able to show others how to face problems and deal with everyday issues.

In football, as in any sport, the leader works harder than the others and makes them believe in an "idea". When they look into your eyes, they have to trust what you say; that is the key to achieving the goal as a team, as a group, and as a family. At this point, you know that you don't have to be worried about others' work; you just need to focus on your work, because you trust in your "brothers" and you know one hundred percent that each one of them is doing their part of the work.

Extra comment/thought/feeling:
A person can be born with greater ability than another but being a "leader" is achieved through work, experience and what you are willing to give for the objective.

CHAPTER 5

Experiences

Experience is gained in two ways; with the passage of time, and by living an intense life. The first is simple; everyone has it if they can live for years. The second is more difficult and requires living a life based on goals and objectives. The cohesion of both will make you have a totally full life. These experiences are what make us what we are, feel what we feel and give back what we have learnt to the people around us.

Is it necessary to leave your hometown to get a more "real-life" experience?

For the author, the answer is yes. Going out of your hometown is not just leaving a physical place, but leaving a context, with the same people, culture, way of life, etc. To live in another context enriches who you are and what you believe in. Even going through bad times, alone or with someone, makes you grow. Life is not easy, and we have to learn that not everything will always be easy and comfortable, as we are living in a tough world where sometimes you can't get any help, advice or protection. These moments make us stronger and, from here, and with that experience, we can transmit things to those who come from behind; we can transmit those experiences and make people understand how to deal with them.

We are talking about using these experiences to help others but also to help ourselves. Everything must serve as learning. When someone plans to take a risk, we should be happy for him/her, because we can lead his/her motivation to the top and then be helpful. Our own experiences could help others not to make the same mistakes or could lead them to achieve great things. We only live once and we need to be open-minded and aware of the power we have in this life.

Learning from experiences, good and bad, depends solely on you. When something good or bad happens, you must analyse it and know that you have done well or badly and improve. It's like planning; you must write down everything that happens to you so that it will serve you for the next time. An experience is just another memory to put into your mind and your heart, but it should be valued at the highest level. What we are, in terms of personality, and how we are with the people around us, it's all part of the same tale, our tale, our history in this world. Letting things go by without acquiring and using what we have learned is a waste of time. It is useless and only makes us waste our time because there is no excuse for falling repeatedly into making the same mistakes; it is your fault for not following good planning and personal analysis.

EXPERIENCE – ANALYSIS – PLAN – ACQUISITION - IMPROVEMENT

First comes the experience, then the analysis of what has happened, and then the plan to assimilate it. Then, once you know it, you are acquiring and internalizing it, but it takes time, and that is when you have improved.

To share what we have been through in life is not a bad thing; it just helps others in taking the right path with better knowledge and a better attitude. The experience doesn't serve just us, it also serves others, because we are here for ourselves and for the people we love.

Freedom and experience walk the same road, because when you are aware that you can get whatever you want and you feel that you have "control" of your life, then you are free; you can feel it in your heart and soul. So, don't be afraid to go for it, to try things, to chase whatever you want to get in this life. Life is too short for being worried about lies and fears that come from others, not from you. But always learn from what you have lived and use it - don't be lazy - learn what you must improve and be better for yourself and for those around you.

Extra comment/thought/feeling:
Sarah Whitaker
Teacher in the United Kingdom. British Department for Education.

Resilience. Resilience isn't about toughness or having a hard exterior. It isn't about having all the answers, and it isn't about repeating your failures over and over again. Resilience is about growing, reflecting, and adapting. We mustn't fear failure, because failure is the key to resilience - and resilience is the key to success.

The key to successful resilience is reflection. When we fall, we must spend some time on the ground reflecting on what it was that brought us there. Did we make the wrong choice? Did we lack a skill? Did we execute a skill in the wrong way? Only when we reflect can we bounce back stronger - and it is through that newly found strength that we develop resilience. Next time you fall, you will remember how it helped you to reflect, to grow and to succeed once again. Only then will you embrace falling and failing. You will see failure as a privilege that helps you to grow and become the best version of you.

In a moment of failure, we must become analysts; strategists; critical thinkers. We must look at these moments through a lens which is totally removed of ambition, ego, and emotion in order to objectively deconstruct how and where we went wrong. We must treat ourselves, our teachers, and our teammates as pieces in a chess game. It is never the piece's fault for the failure - it was the move

Experiences

that failed. Were the pieces moved in the wrong sequence? Did one particular move leave you vulnerable? Did you have a strategy prepared when you started playing in the first instance? Being able to identify the weak spots in our play leaves us better prepared for the same chess game in the future. Instead, if you wallow in your failure to win that chess game and beat yourself up for being a terrible chess player, you'll continue to make the same mistakes in the future - or maybe more. By reflecting on that failed chess game, you can make positive changes that will, in turn, help you to win. And in winning, we embrace the next time that we fail - because that's what made us better in the first place.

This is the real meaning of resilience - seeing failure as the real win.

CHAPTER 6

The Fear

When we talk about fear, various synonyms and feelings come to our mind, like terror, loneliness, helplessness, cold, prejudice, panic, horror, alarm, fright, shock, suspicion, apprehension, distrust, embarrassment, surprise, astonishment, cowardice, etc.

The fear is the fear of life, of the unknown; why do you get up one day with energy and other days you don't feel the same? We are talking about feelings, about the dreams that we had, have, and will have, about this life that goes so quick and sometimes doesn't let us follow it. It is so hard to live in this world, but we try to do it every day and, in the end, we get it because we don't need to control everything. Becoming aware of that takes years, but finally, you will discover your own happy world.

There are many types of fear, and all are related to our own fears, and even some that we create ourselves. Fear is a dangerous companion, but sometimes, it is even good because it makes you have "respect" for certain things, and makes you stay alert. But generally, it is not a good companion, because it prevents you from relating to the environment in a normal way. It makes you live things in a different way, and, without a doubt, it makes you miss interesting things in life.

There are many times when fear is caused by us. We think that people are speaking badly of us or that they are going to do something really bad to us, but the reality is that nobody really thinks badly of you and you have the same options as everyone to get things, but you hurt yourself with negative thoughts. It would be interesting to know where this comes from. Above all, it comes from a total lack of confidence in yourself and in how you relate to your environment. Therefore, you are building yourself a "wall", which only hurts yourself. It doesn't make sense, but it happens continuously.

Once, a friend told me: "Fear is a barrier that we put up ourselves and that prevents us from progressing in ideas or actions that we want to do." As we said before, it is very true that sometimes, we have bad feelings about people saying bad things about us, which is just not true but we create and invent things in our minds. Ninety percent of the thoughts or prejudices that we have come from us, not from true thoughts, and these kinds of ideas make us fall into a negative dynamic, and this is called "fear", sensations that do not allow us to move on and forward, to be able to be free to do whatever we feel or desire. The day that we understand that we are our own "wall" will be the day when we will not be afraid to risk and to fight for the things that we want and love, delivering all the confidence and passion.

Fear and confidence depend on your context and how you see the things that happen around you. As we said before, ten percent is what happens to you and the other ninety percent is how you face it. It is something you learn over time; nothing and no one is perfect, but it can be, if you just let yourself go and do what you can to live without worrying too much about the context, or anything in general, just living in a healthy way with you and others around.

Fear comes from many sides but especially from oneself, because, in the end, it all begins and ends in us. If you find the halfway point between wisdom and madness, you can get to do great things and live this time in a free and passionate way.

Many times, fear comes from feeling lost, because we don't have control, or we just control fifty percent of the things that we want to control. We just need to focus on the fact that we don't control the context and we will never be able to do it, so we must be organized and effective in what we do, solving the problems we have, but not worry too much about everything because it will destroy us.

We recommend focusing on these easy steps:

"Confidence"

-Trusting your feelings means knowing where you want to go. It comes from the security transmitted and acquired by our context and experiences since childhood, the relationship with our parents, and friends, and bad and good experiences. From there comes an idea that chooses a path for each one of us. From here, we ask for help and advice from those who want to help us to find that path that we often cannot see. On the other hand, embrace the isolation, because she is the only one in her darkness that will make you see truly who you are.

"Value your own experience"

-This is a key rule - if you do not value yourself, who will do it? It is good to sit at a table and think about what you have done wrong and well in life, because no one is perfect, and we need to accept who we are in order to improve. Be aware that everyone around you wants the same thing as you, and the people that have fears or doubts about themselves will complain about others and will not look at themselves first. People who know what they are and the value that they have, do not need the approval of others. So, it's not normal for people to go against you if you make your own life, because there is a lot of jealousy in this world. Be ready to counterattack. Firstly, though, value who you are and focus on improving yourself. Another piece of advice is to do things right away; do not wait. We talk about living for today as tomorrow may never come, so don't be lazy.

"Short life"

-I once heard a stockbroker say, "Retire; the game is overrated". Work for a while, work hard for your personal and professional goals, but when you can be stable and able to enjoy, enjoy and live, have no fear. Living is really not easy and not everyone is prepared to do it. You have to be brave to really live because humans will always be asked about where we come from and where we are going. We need a balance between duties and pleasure, but sometimes, we just focus on the duties and that makes life miserable. To be brave in order to live a real life is hard and not many people have succeeded with it, but we definitely need to try. Realize that we will all die, so we cannot always be worried; we must live and try to smile.

"Learn from experience"

-There is nothing more important and definitive when it comes to leading your business than recalling good and bad experiences and remembering what you can improve. Even so, sometimes, because we are all human beings, you will fall back into failure but be aware of them and that will put you on alert. Life and success are summarized in two headings - common sense and experience - plus a little bit of luck.

Extra comment/thought/feeling:
Hugo Guillén Asensio
HR Manager professional.

In general, fear is a natural reaction to uncertain or dangerous situations. When I went to Slovakia the first time, I had to have courage and overcome fear, perhaps a little recklessly. I did not know that area of Europe before, but I informed myself and made sure in some way that it would go well. Another experience; when I went to study an Erasmus in Germany, it was the first time that I had spent so much time outside of Spain, so, at first, I was a little scared, which is normal, but then you get used to it; you learn the language, you integrate very fast with other Erasmus students, and you have a great time. So, the following year, instead of wanting to return to Spain, I continued in Germany with another exchange program in another city, and, in the third year, moved to another with another internship on the Erasmus program. Whenever you change cities, fear and uncertainty appear, but after time, you get used to it, and you also get over it with the desire to learn new things, the language, new people, new places, etc.

Then there is a fear of being alone too. For example, I spent time in a city in northern Germany called Rinteln, which was more of a town, and although the school where I worked had a good atmosphere, I had to live quite alone and isolated for a time. It was quite a painful experience, and I would say that the best way to overcome that fear is to do activities, even if it is playing football or tennis with people or signing up for things. It is common when you change cities, etc., but I have friends and I know Spanish people who have had similar problems in Germany or Poland, etc., which are colder places.

Returning to the topic of fear; when I went to Bratislava to work at Amazon, fear was also inevitable when having to face such a big change, but the motivation to both grow professionally, and to learn something new and be with the person you wanted, that's what really makes you overcome everything; achieving the goals you have and not putting any walls around yourself. Life is easier than we think but there are many times when we are the ones who make it more difficult.

CHAPTER 7

Goals in Life

We must value two types of goals – personal and professional.

On a professional level, we need goals, something that makes us try to improve, feel good, that allows us to give value to our lives, and something in which we can leave something for the future, a good legacy. Imagine a life without goals, without doing anything, without wanting to improve or be good at something, without tastes other than a comfortable life. Surely there will be many people with me, who think they do not want that kind of life. Having professional goals also affects a personal level, because it gives you a "reason" to live, to move forward, no matter what happens.

There is a subgroup within the professional goals that are linked to passion, like football which is your job but your passion at the same time. There, your football team is your family, a group of people with special personalities, and even if sometimes you don't agree on everything or you experience bad situations, you all fight for the same cause because football " is your life and passion". It is the only passion and goal that makes you feel alive. It is difficult to say if this feeling for a job is good or bad; for some, it is a good thing, because it gives meaning to their life. For others, the opposite, because it means you do not have time to do other things, such as expanding your social life. But, when your job is your passion, you do not see work as an obligation, it is what you like. You are passionate about it; it is what you want to dedicate yourself to and where you want to spend your time.

Any passion for something, with a good balance, can give precious meaning to your life. We must value it and know that this passion is born from within, from the dedication and belief in something more important than your life, and that it offers you sensations and a loyalty that cannot be explained.

For a footballer, this type of goal is essential. You have to love it a lot, but it is not talking about it, it is demonstrated with the daily actions: How you take care of yourself, how you train, eat, drink, sleep, how you listen more than speak, demonstrate more than say and focus on the goal more than distractions. A footballer must be very careful of the context, as there will be many people wanting many things from you. You must be focused on how important it is to train and learn; the rest of the things do not matter. Listen to your trusted people and do not change your way of being or your goals for material things; be humble and love the game; be happy with it, that is the key.

That feeling of being complete, of feeling the "struggle", the effort with which great things are achieved, there is nothing like it; and once you feel it, you won't stop loving it. Let this spirit enter you, dominate you, and if you know how to direct it, "you will be truly alive." The more it costs, the better the victory tastes.

On a personal level, we must try to achieve the most precious asset of all, which is happiness. We must not allow professional goals to sacrifice happiness; having a balance is essential. We could write a list of objectives that human beings can describe as goals to achieve in life, but happiness is the most precious of them all.

Chasing the goals that make us feel good is tough. Often, we are guided by goals that do not come from us, they come from our parent's desires, or are made by the brands, or TV since we are young. It is not easy to know if what I want or like comes from me or is directed by the context. This has always been a concern of modern "philosophers and writers", how much we are conditioned by context and how to try not to be.

Goals in Life

We must look within ourselves at our experiences and remember what we like. The professional side is not everything, but it helps if you like your job because we spend a lot of time working. Your personal life should be an important thing in your life, and we must try to surround ourselves with people who treat us well and make us grow and feel calm in life; people who love us for who we are and not for what we have.

One of the most important goals for many people is to find a partner. Speaking of relationships, there will be people who only want "someone" to accompany them in their life, they will not care if it is you or someone else. Personally, I think you must try to get away from these people. It is better to be truly loved, and that they love you rather than someone else. You must find a person that loves you and respects how you are and together, make that project of life in common, where you both sacrifice yourselves for the other and give everything for that project in common. Through trust, respect and love you can achieve the goals together.

The important thing is that alone or accompanied, we need to have goals in life; otherwise, life is meaningless. To choose them well and have a good balance between them is difficult, but that's the difference between a good or bad life. Therefore, there are many types of goals in life, but the most important thing is to have them, and, above all, that they make you happy. Also, trying to have a "passion" for something, sacrificing and having effort for something is very beautiful and will give meaning to your life. We have the possibility of living a life full of experiences and adventures, so do not let anyone, not even yourself, take you away from this; find what you want and go for it with freedom and full of confidence.

Extra comment/thought/feeling:
The final goal is important, but it is all the way we have travelled that makes our lives unique and special.

CHAPTER 8

Organization

Organization consists of planning, analyzing, and carrying out a series of actions, with little effort, that makes your life much easier and under control. Organization is subject to decision-making and an attitude towards life and the problems that arise in it. A good organization requires work prior to action, but then you just must follow the plan, so it will save a lot of time.

Having order in your life will give you the balance you need, it will take away stress, and it will free you from mistakes and problems. It just takes having the ability to analyze what you need and taking control of your life.

Organization is the basis of life; something organized will make you live more calmly with yourself and your environment. Everything in this life depends on decisions. Decision-making is complicated and difficult because the context in which you are making the decision is sometimes hard, so it creates insecurity, even more so if you are alone. We must make decisions based on facts, our thoughts and the context that surrounds us. Try not to decide with your heart because it's not useful, although I understand that sometimes it is easier to do than deciding based on real life. However, the decisions must be clear and must be made with respect to a plan, having previously analyzed them and, in addition, having both a Plan B and a Plan C as backup. We must never let a moment of madness or the heart direct our way; feelings are useful, but we must stick to the plan as much as possible, and for that, order is key. The important things require analysis, organization and decision-making based on a plan.

Our thoughts are forged according to a multitude of things - our past, present, advice from friends or simply by impulses according to a lived experience. The context at the time of making decisions is key, because, as we will see in the chapter where we talk about "the context", it unintentionally conditions us and we must try to dominate and control it. We cannot let impulses, sensations and other people condition our lives, as it is down to us to take control of our own lives.

Organization gives you order and brings serenity and balance to the mind, allowing you to make decisions in the best way. Deciding depends on the mix of two factors - a thought you have at that moment, along with the vision you have of the context at that precise moment. The context will always condition us in our decision. In addition, the context is very changeable; as much as we do, we think one thing when we sleep and another thing when we wake up, according to what we feel and see. But when you live with a pre-established order, you have a better chance of making the correct decisions because you will not be so conditioned by what you feel at that moment.

The reality of life is that as much as you make a decision thinking about all the factors, you may be wrong. But that's the way life is and it's not going to change, so it is key to make the decision and then do two things. The first is that when you make a decision, recognise that it has already been made, have enough personality to carry it out, don't think about it anymore, and do not be worried about what happens because what has to come will come. Secondly, what we can and should do is prepare ourselves to face several of the things that may happen, to be fully prepared no matter what. To plan something, whatever it is, we need to be organised and we need to have our minds clear and ready to face different situations and contexts. We cannot blame life because it cannot do anything for you; you are the master of your destiny because, in the end, we can get whatever we want to.

Order is the foundation of a good life, as it makes us effective and efficient in our efforts. Spending five minutes making a good plan could help to stop you from wasting hours. Our own biology makes us try to expend as little energy as possible and save the energy that we have. This happens in all aspects of life, and we must be the ones to work hard in order to achieve this order.

Order is the best weapon for the "lazy" person who does not want to make any effort. You have to think that the more orderly you are, the less effort you will expend, the fewer round-trip tasks you will have to do, etc. It's just smarter to be orderly but it takes time to know it and be aware of it.

It is important to understand that in this world there are many dangers in the form of companies, people, countries, etc. It is necessary to keep control of your possessions every day. Without order, the stress levels will be much higher, but if you are tidy, everything will be better and more controlled for the benefit of your own health.

Chaos does not benefit anyone, and in this case, not even yourself, so if you want to be calmer, organize your life:

-**Analyse** what you need
-**Forget** what you DO NOT need
-**Control** what you DO need
-**Organize** the day to day

Order is as simple as leaving things in the place that you found them previously. You do not have to do crazy things or think too much about anything, you just have to live from normality and simplicity.

There are some people against it because they think that to have order means to lose your freedom, but order is just a quality that makes your life easier, and I cannot understand why people don't see it.

Order brings the balance in your life necessary to buy time and not waste it with nonsense. It is up to you if you wish to succeed or not, but the best decisions are always taken from control, tranquillity, and balance, and it is order that brings you all those.

Extra comment/thought/feeling:
Being always ready and prepared is not difficult; it only requires order and mental and physical stability. If you are not prepared, failure will be waiting for you.

CHAPTER 9

Business = Relations

Business is just a commercial exchange, and the reality is that everything depends on personal relationships; nothing more. Whatever happens in a business deal depends on the relations between parties because we are talking about people, trust, and values. It all depends on the relations between clients and the trust within that group of people and companies. We will talk about "trust" in another chapter in this book, but we have to say that we cannot trust people just for how they talk or the feeling that comes from the first meeting. This process of "commercial relationships of trust" requires improvement and experience.

Relationships are everything, because we are social beings who need to "touch" with others, and we appreciate it. It is inevitable that the human being behaves like a "sociable" being; that's how we are, and we carry it inside. So, it is inevitable that we help or favour our friends or people with whom we share common interests. We are surrounded by interests, and the business world is no different. Everything is moved by the interest of people with common goals, and it is normal because we will never stop having "our animal side" when it comes to protecting our goals, our survival and improvement. What has made human beings dominate the other animals on the planet has been our desire to create, be better, improve, invent, etc.

We must differentiate personal relationships from interpersonal ones. The first are directed to love; friendships that are more related to relationships, and the second are directed to emotions and feelings of business, laws, or social manners. In business relationships, both have a place, since, at an interpersonal level, we must all maintain form and manners, however, it is on a personal level where you can get the good deals and contracts.

On the other hand, it is important to talk about the word "business", a word that has been reviled many times by a part of society that qualifies it as something "bad, harmful and dark", when doing business is simply based on agreements where jobs are often created, and the economy moves smoothly. We must not let behaviours or social fantasies make us reveal ourselves to the "creation" of things, in this case, business.

We have to highlight an important thing about the personality that we need to have in the business world. People will respect you if you are tough, not if you are bad. Be honest but be tough and fight for your interests. People will respect you for your actions. Nobody wants to associate with a weak person; they will say that you are a good person but they will never respect you and you need respect to establish a good path for you. The most important thing is to be honest, open, and sociable but when the time comes, tough, relentless, and guarding your interests and those of the group above all else. Knowing how to earn the respect of others will make other people want to join you because they will see that they can trust you to "fight" for your/their business.

Communication, relations, teamwork, and a strong personality are the four keys to a good professional life:

"Communication"

-The key to being able to work without any problems of misunderstandings or issues; Also, the key to building relations with the people around you, to know them, to feel what they feel and know what they know. The communication process is based on the trust and harmony of a relationship between two or more people, so we must make sure that we do all we can to make it real and easy.

"Relations"

-Being social means building relations and knowing people in an easy way; if we have this characteristic, we will find many good things in return, because being able to meet people and share experiences is the key for future professional/personal business.

"Teamwork"

-To be open enough to create good partnerships with people that you don't know personally is a very important key to creating a good atmosphere and synergising to get the professional target that all of you have in common.

"Strong Personality"

-People will respect you when you make yourself respected. Nobody wants someone weak at their side in a business. Being honest and open is key but you also must be tough and fight for your interests and those of the group. In this way, people will trust you because if they see that you care about yourself, they know that you will also care about their interests in the case of a common business/ goal.

Achieving what we want relies on our personal and professional skills. Many people think that professional skills should be the foundation to building a good career, but the real thing is that everything in this world is managed by your personal skills and how you socialize with people and that is the key for your life as well as for growing as a professional. Building relationships is the key to developing a business and growing in life; it all depends on it.

Extra comment/thought/feeling:
You must be careful because good things are very hard to get but losing them is achieved very quickly due to carelessness or false understanding.

CHAPTER 10

The Peace

Inner peace is the foundation of everything. Peace is not sought; it's expected, lived and achieved. The less you realize of it, the more you will find it; it doesn't need to be pursued. Peace is not bought, not jealous, not selfish; it only finds you effortlessly, but with a prior process on a personal level.

There are many stages in life and a thousand ways to live each one of them, so it is difficult to find what you want in every moment of life, but if you feel good and you are positive, it is easier to get to what we call "peace". I do not speak of happiness because it implies a certain moment; peace, in my opinion, is the feeling of knowing who you are, where you are and where you are going, and feeling good about it. Happiness only comes and is felt at certain times, but peace is something we either have or don't have. There are days that are peaceful and days that are not, but, at the end of the day, if we have done what we should, it will find us because it is related to the relationship that we have with ourselves.

Peace means to be at peace with oneself; to look in the mirror and feel that you respect yourself for your life. It is very difficult to be at peace with oneself because you also must be at peace with your surroundings. It is difficult to control oneself because of the context in which we live and that of people who live their own lives as well. There are many people who do not care about us at all, and there will even be some who want to hurt us, so we must be aware of this, but they should never make us lose our "balance".

Balance is based on us and our context, but, above all, on how we feel about ourselves and at the same time, how we relate to the environment; how we feel about it. To have peace is the sum of several concepts that can be summed up in the self-respect that every human being must have for himself/herself and the emotional stability that comes from his/her effective social and working life.

Is it possible to build the balance we are talking about?

The hard part is to achieve peace, but we must try to build it. Build it from the knowledge of oneself and the clear target of what you want in life. Context is important, but trying to control it is almost impossible. Being patient can build a life that allows you to enjoy the day-to-day with a context that sometimes will add positive things and sometimes negative things. The balance where peace comes from is achieved with effort, positivity, and patience - they are the three keys, and we must have a balance between them to achieve it.

Many people say that peace cannot find you because you must find it. I believe that it can be built, but at the same time, it can come in an unplanned way. What is true is that you have to be prepared to know how to understand and recognize when peace has come to you and be brave enough to take it and not let it go, because we live once, and the rest of history doesn't matter.

To be clear-minded and free enough from past thoughts to pursue your targets is the most important thing and the only thing that you must care about. It is called "consciousness" and appears when something in the past persecutes us and does not stop. The peace that we can have is disturbed at that time because there is something that interferes. It is not good to leave it, but it is better to seek treatment and talk to people of confidence or even a professional. Saving and locking things inside of us could be worse for our health and destroy us in the future. Without doubt, telling someone what we feel is necessary to be able to live a pure life. Patience, analysis and making our thoughts real will help us to go step by step toward our goals and will preserve calm and well-being.

When you are aware of how to win or lose, that is the moment when you must make decisions about what you really want to do. We cannot analyse this fact from any example, because we all understand that there are many examples that come from winning and losing. The truth is that the ego, chasing impossible things and believing that winning is the only thing that makes you alive, is another stupid fact. We should not let false egos take us away from what is important, such as family, quality of life, knowledge, etc. Spending time in our job or on something that we need because we must do it is understandable, but we always need to have the option to change that path to another. Be in the position to be able to make decisions and change your life when you desire; that's the greatest victory.

We need to love our life, and we must do stuff that sometimes is not the best thing in that moment; we do it for money or duty. However, we need to take control of our lives and not let the ego take over. The most important things in life are family, friends, working at something that you like, and, in the end, just being happy and the ego will never lead you there.

Ego can be useful sometimes because we need to have great ideas to succeed in life, but we need to ask ourselves what is the greatest thing that we can achieve, and the answer is peace and happiness. Ego can lead you to achieve great things and to feel happiness for a while, but never mistake those feelings for the feeling of a group of friends, or home. Balance, happiness, and peace are not just words, they are needs and we need to get them for our life.

Extra comment/thought/feeling:
Manuel Pérez Cascallana
UEFA Pro Licence football coach. Assistant Coach Persib Bandung (Indonesia Super League). Former Club Atlético de

The Things We Know and Do Not Say

Madrid, and former Assistant Coach ATK FC from the Indian Super League. Winner of the Indian Super League Trophy, season 2019/20.

Inner peace is the most important goal of happiness that we have because in order to have relationships with other individuals, firstly we must feel good about ourselves and that is why we have the need to know ourselves.

For me, inner peace means feeling calm with yourself knowing that you have tried everything that was within your reach to achieve your GOAL.

First of all, we should not feel guilty when we find some time for ourselves, to know ourselves, and not feel bad about thinking that we are doing something non-productive.

There is the error; of course, it is productive and for the personal benefit of each individual. That is what we must change in our mentality, which assumes that it is only productive if it generates economic interest.

The free man is the person who chooses his path in life. All of us at some point in time have felt free to decide, however difficult it may be, feeling comfortable with ourselves knowing that we have made the right decision even though it may affect or harm other people.

An indication of the term inner peace can be found at night in our house, at the moment that we conclude our day and begin to think about what happened during it. If the day has been PRODUCTIVE, the individual feels more "inner peace" in his body, which is nothing more than an emotional reinforcement to know that, according to your criteria, you have done things well, or at least, as you think they should be done.

Buddhist culture has always been a religion that caught my attention, since it constantly talks about the states of the mind, and promoting happiness based on self-control, balance and inner peace.

Currently, there are psychological theories that have as their purpose the self-control and emotional management of the individual, two characteristics closely linked to inner peace that form the "theme" that we are individuals.

According to Dr Alan Wallace, a good mental predisposition when facing realities can help us deactivate our negative thoughts, and for this, we must look for lifelong, medium and short-term purposes to find meaning in our days, motivating ourselves constantly to improve ourselves.

The older you are, the more experience you have acquired on your back, and that is why, according to Jacques Philippe, in his book "Inner Peace", experience is a good indicator to trust so as not to make the same mistakes.

Although we all know the importance of the mind in the human being, very few in-depth studies can be found on it.

The question should now be: How do we achieve inner peace?

CHAPTER 11

Love, Help, Selfishness

There are many interests in this life; interests as an individual, as a member of a group, personal interests, professionals, etc. Each one of us has a life, targets for which we have to interact and relate to others. There are frictions and problems, but good things also happen; people help each other, and we share our life with others.

Love, helping and not being selfish are three concepts to mix into one. The key in life is to love and help those who deserve it, and not be selfish with those who don't deserve it either. We will always meet good and bad people in this world, so we should know the person first and then give our love; also, we need to create and forge our own personality, with values and a conviction for being good, but not being stupid and always analysing the environment to make decisions.

When we talk about "helping", we are talking about a characteristic of the person, never helping too much or too little, because helping someone who needs and deserves it has no limit. We must help because we are sociable human beings; no one can do all things alone, so we need to be open enough in order to get love and company as well. If you need help, it does not mean necessarily that you are weak, because every human being needs to talk to someone, listen, see, feel; it is as simple as that. In addition, the sum of efforts will help yourself and others to improve both professionally and personally.

"Help without asking for anything in return"

Love, Help, Selfishness

This is a key and difficult point that many people experience because it is strictly related to not being selfish. Give what you don't need, give what you have, that is the spirit of "social" life as a group, and as a sport, football helps in this part.

In football, all these characteristics are given and fulfilled. Within a group, you must love, help and not be selfish; this reinforces the "group" against the "individual". The team will never win for the individual, only if it is a "family". The team will build and lay the foundations for top players to show their level in key situations, but "only with good foundations can the house be built." The captain is a key piece; the captain must command, lead by example, and help the staff to solve problems. A united group is unstoppable, and each member of the group has their role in achieving this.

However, not everything in life is easy, nor are we all the same, nor do we all think the same. Everyone is selfish at some point; we are animals and it is normal to think about ourselves. We seek the best for ourselves and the ones we love, to live as best as possible. We show love to people, and we also help people, but sometimes it's not for love or help, it's just because we want to socialize, and indirectly, we are being selfish and just want to do some stuff in order to feel better about ourselves. Sometimes we do not even realise this fact; we try to be good and show respect or friendship, but we do not like that person in particular, it's just a pure feeling of selfishness, but as I said, we are not aware of it and it is normal to happen.

It is human to act like that sometimes. We don't deserve to get embarrassed for it because we cannot control all the actions and feelings that we express. We just need to try to help, love and be there for the good people that we know. If we are aware that we are being selfish and that person does not deserve it, realizing and doing nothing makes us bad people, and this must be avoided at all costs. Preserving inner purity is something that you cannot lose because the person who cannot look in the mirror and feel good about himself/herself is not on the right track.

Now, it's time to talk about the love in a relationship; the love that you feel for another person in order to share a life together.

How do you know if it's true love?

Life has tests ready for all of us that let you know if it's true or not. The idea of love is beautiful but once a certain time has passed, the doubts arrive, so only what you feel and see has value, because the rest does not count. Follow or not, the feelings depend on the heart. There is no reason, no thoughts, nothing better or worse, just you alone with him/her feeling great for being with the best person in the world. If you do not feel that, in my opinion, you should take another path because it doesn't have a future, but if that feeling really comes out and it's real, you should deliver all you've got. "Love" - it is beautiful, but, at the same time, so dark and mysterious.

Love should also be based on being compatible as a couple because loving is helping each other, it is helping each other to improve as a couple and individually, in all aspects of life. Being with someone implies effort and growing together.

There are a lot of lies about the word love, and there are many relationships that are only based on the interest of being accompanied, of being with someone, but that is not love. There are many people who only want to be accompanied; that is not love and we must try to find someone who really is for us, who means something to us. Something real is better than something invented and it is always better to be alone than with someone that just doesn't want to be alone. There are many couples today with this problem. They are together just because they didn't find their real love. In my opinion, this is something that will not last because even if we try to use the mind, love comes from the heart and by deeds in the day-to-day.

These three words are united - love, help and selfishness. Love is born from the need to feel alive and close to another person, but everything is based on helping each other, on making the path of life together. Love is to accompany the other person, to share everything, to feel that you have another person next to you that you can trust and can improve and progress with in life.

Sometimes we should admit that we will be doing things not for helping or loving, but because we are selfish, and we need it for our ego or even for survival. Therefore, love exists, but the line between love and being selfish is thin. We should love and be loved, so we should remember this and try to choose the right people to share life with.

The reality of life is that everything depends on having a balance. A good personal balance will help you in your professional life, and vice versa, but the personal always comes first as the foundation of your personality. If you are honest and have good values, and you know the good and bad in the world, you will be able to understand a phrase that will mark your life.

"Sow and reap"

If you sow (give and help), good things will happen to you and people will help you back in the same way. But do not give without analysing and knowing to whom you are giving, because otherwise you will be stupid, and people will take advantage of you.

"Balance is key in life"

Extra comment/thought/feeling:
Aurora Morales
Teacher in Spain. Spanish Department for Education.

To me, being open-minded is not being prejudiced against people, and that is very difficult. I know; it costs. And since I often have prejudices, for different reasons, I do my best to try to know and understand them. Thus, on many occasions, my way of thinking has changed. Others don't do this, so I try not to attach labels, not to judge ... before knowing more about something.

Selfless is basically not being selfish. Selfishness is our greatest "sin". We need to think that we are just one person; we are nothing without the rest. You must think more about others. Do not go with the "I always"; be part of the people, of your people, and support each other.

Person, human being, humanity ... They are simple words, or they have a real and valuable meaning. What does it mean to be a person, to be a human being? At the legal or biological level, they have a clear and concrete meaning. But when this is not what interests us, it can be more complicated.

Perhaps, at first, we are interested in talking about people as members of a large group rather than referring to one person individually. This is because each one of us is part of a great community that is Humanity.

And among so many, a single person may not seem important. But it's not like that. What each person is and does matters. Sure, it matters. What each of us is and does adds up, like infinite grains of sand, to form something very big.

And on a day-to-day basis, however, it is not necessary to think so much about that great whole, Humanity. Because with large numbers, with great things, we run the risk of losing ourselves and it becomes easy to find excuses not to act and not to feel involved and for believing it to be useless.

All of us, the vast majority, are members of some community, or several. A community of neighbours, an office, a factory, a school, a family, a town, a sports team ... And it is here, in short distances, where the person takes on a special meaning.

As human beings, we are, or must at least try to be responsible, active, tolerant, generous and brave. And the feeling, among others, that can lead us to achieve it is love. The love of another, and not in the general sense of loving Humanity. It is about love and good work towards who you have close to you - your brother, your friend, your neighbour, your partner ...

So, from one to another and from another to one ... like a chain, finally, love can reach people, and come back to you.

As the Beatles say in a song:

"And in the end, the love you take is equal to the love you make."

CHAPTER 12

Loneliness

Loneliness can be positive or negative depending on how it is handled and the balance that it has. It can be positive because it helps to know oneself and negative because we human beings are social beings and we need contact with other people, and it is not good to be always alone; it could destroy the person.

Managing your thoughts means being in control of what you feel. Having positive thoughts in a period of loneliness is something fundamental, which will make you think about the positivity of loneliness rather than the negativity. We must know ourselves and know how to manage our feelings and what we need and never fall into negative thoughts that imply thinking about the bad things of the context. Negativity will make us think about the lack of company, love and friendship, which will destroy our internal world.

The key is to manage loneliness by bringing out the good in it and not falling into the bad that it could be because it can be very bad if you sink into it. Being alone with oneself is very complicated because we have many thoughts where there are always many questions with no answer. The action of asking ourselves and answering ourselves in loneliness can be beneficial for many people, but also very harmful for other types of people. We can reach a sense of introspection where you can get to know yourself better and come out stronger. However, there are people who cannot stand loneliness, not being able to discuss or argue, and not feeling anything from another;

there are even people who need confrontation with other people as a daily routine.

There are many people who only find happiness or calm in solitude. Being alone undoubtedly helps you to know yourself more, to know what you want, and if you can do it outside a big city, it is even better, away from the noise and all civilization, to be able to calm your body and your mind. A period of loneliness can strengthen your mind to realize what you need, what you want, and who you are; it is where the greats find creativity, away from adverts, brands, people, etc. that do nothing but send messages to our minds and do not let us think clearly.

Therefore, it is good for the health to be alone sometimes. It's good because you can understand much better your feelings, regrets, and all you want to be and not be. Human beings should have times when they just focus on themselves and think about their lives and where they are going. Loneliness is not bad; loneliness purifies, encourages, gives strength, and unites what you are. It is interesting to realize all the noises that are around, but when you are in a place where it is quiet and you don't have any duties to care about, then you can listen to yourself - you feel the "peace". This sense of peace means getting energy, and it's healthy. It is a thing that we should experience more often.

Loneliness can be useful, as we said, but at the same time, it can destroy you if you cross the boundaries, because in the end, we are humans and we need to socialize. Loneliness can lead to depression or disorders due to a lack of interaction with other people, especially at an early age and in adolescence. That is why we talk about having a balance, knowing how to measure and calibrate the degree of loneliness we have. It is fundamental because we live in a global world where we must know how to manage relationships.

It makes me wonder. How do I find myself?

It's a question with no answer but what is clear is that being negative is never going to help anything or anyone, so you must use solitude in a good way, where being alone for a while helps you to find yourself positively, placed in an elevated position and makes us confront our deepest ideas. Let's hear what these ideas have to say; we will find good and bad things, but the reality will benefit us more than it will harm us.

It is also true that social networks are opening us to new worlds and people but changing the way in which people communicate and relate, so on a psychological level, it was necessary to study how these changes in trends and ways of relating to each other affect us on a personal and professional level.

Let's focus this topic on the world of football and a young player, who is the type of player to whom this book is directed. We imagine a Spanish player from Cádiz, for example, who, at the age of 18, signs a contract to play with the English team Derby County in the Midlands. We are talking about very different contexts and where loneliness can be a key piece in the player's performance.

In this topic, we must look at several variables: Different countries, therefore, the different cultures that this implies, a different way of being, feeling, relating, interacting between people, eating, and having fun; even when celebrating a goal, it is shouted in a different way. When you change country or city, apart from the above, you do not have your friends and family, therefore, you lose that closeness with who you feel are your immediate contacts. The language is different, and this change is important because you lose the ability to relate and communicate in the way you are used to. You lose something that you have essentially had since you were young, which makes you that person. We are talking about a very big change on an individual and social level.

How do we face this change and what factors will be key to facing the loneliness that you may suffer?

The first and most important thing is to be positive, as positivity helps us create good feelings and having good feelings makes us feel better. From there, creating a new context that favours what you want and long for is vital. This implies making friends, making plans, adapting to the country but continuing with certain traditional customs of yours, and above all, not losing contact with your people. Work also helps you have a goal, and creating professional goals opens a range of possibilities where you can keep your mind busy.

There are many cases of footballers who do not adapt to the country or the context and have to return home or don't show their best performance. Now, it happens less and less, since we have all understood that we live in a world where to stay in our home cities forever is not the norm anymore.

We don't need to fear what we feel or the deepest ideas that we have because we will need all of them in order to improve as human beings.

Extra comment/thought/feeling:
The mind is everything, and it depends on oneself whether it is well or not. It is up to you.

CHAPTER 13

Priorities

Prioritizing some things over others depends on several concepts: needs, interests, obligations, and targets. Priorities may come from a need to eat, an interest in doing something, a moral, social, or monetary obligation to do so, or simply a business or personal goal.

It is difficult to know the reason for other people's decisions because we do not know their background or their reasons for making such decisions. That is why we must always respect and not make judgments about why a person takes one path or another.

Although I would say that the priority that every single human person has is the pursuit of "happiness", we are humans, so we try to complicate our life. It happens because we always want more and don't realize that life is short and maybe we will not have a "tomorrow". So, live your life, strong and intense, make a future, be good but, at the same time, don't forget who you are and who the people are who truly love you, because they're the people you should be with RIGHT NOW, not even reading this book.

We need to differentiate between needs and priorities. Many times, our situation makes us have more needs and we must cover them, rather than having options and being able to choose the order of our priorities. When I have a situation that allows me to choose in which position I put each of the things I do in life, I can prioritize some things over others.

Priorities

Being able to choose what I want and what I don't want to do, and having the "time" to do it, is very important and priceless because the most valuable thing in life is time and being able to have the opportunity to use it however you want.

How do I get into the position of being able to buy time and then choosing what to do with it?

It all depends on the life plan you have, how smart you are over resources and the passion you have to carry it out.

The first thing is to have a plan and organize the steps to take to achieve it, always thinking about the worst that could happen and being realistic in your claims. Then you have to carry it out and make adjustments because conditions change along the way.

Finally, you must dedicate time and know how to obtain the contacts that allow you to have a position of control over the situation that you want to dominate. This requires time, work, having a clear mind and the ability to adapt.

The priority should always be our "happiness" but it depends on the context, which often makes it difficult for us to focus on it exclusively. To have happiness, several important aspects must be linked; our personal, social, and professional life. Each one must be addressed separately and each one in relation to the others. Achieving a balance between all of them will be the key to achieving the ultimate goal, which is happiness. And it is this word "balance" that is the key to everything in this life.

How do priorities relate to having a good balance in life?

These are two different aspects to this - one talks about focusing on something and the other about paying attention to everything. However, happiness is not conceived simply by prioritizing everything over one thing. The word prioritize means having some goals above others but never giving up everything for one thing. So, prioritizing and balance are totally related to our path.

To prioritize happiness, we should only focus on what we want one hundred percent, always adjusting to the plan and adapting to the contexts that occur. Get up and know that you have a goal, that you are following the plan and you feel good about it. That is the greatest feeling that exists in the professional world, and it gives meaning to your life.

Prioritizing in football is a daily occurrence since we are in a business where you can work in one country today, and tomorrow, you must move. This can involve being in relationships with many people, both in the club and while moving. Combining work and personal life is a very recurring theme because the stability of playing in the same club is not something normal, so we talk about many variables that are connected to each other.

How to manage the context and know how to prioritize?

The first thing to understand is that football is a business, and we make a living from it. So, we must fight for our rights as a worker but also accept that there are times when we will not get everything we want.

Professionalism is key and contractual matters must be handled by someone you trust. What you ask must be commensurate with what you offer but always ask for more so even if they offer lower, you get what you want. Prioritizing between work and personal life is a personal choice, but the life of the footballer is short, and you will need that money in the future, so it is time to make sacrifices today to live better tomorrow.

To be focused on your work, control all aspects of it, and surround yourself with good people to help you professionally and personally. Prioritize your physical and mental state above all else; train, eat and rest well but also have fun because balance is key in this circle. Be brave, make yourself respected but also be good to others because you never know who you will need in the future.

Sometimes we forget what really matters because we have expectations from people, we read comments, etc. We may face things we don't really like but we are in a global world with so many options and temptations. How to deal with all of them is important but not easy. Remember that it is not what happens, but how you take it.

My advice is to analyse your life and check if you are truly happy, and if your personal and professional desires are being achieved. If not, something is going wrong and we should have a plan to change. Perhaps even taking some time out could be worthwhile. Your priorities should always be in line with your desires and what you love/like more, so it is important to know your targets then go for them.

Extra comment/thought/feeling:
The priority should always be to enjoy the journey, not to win, but to enjoy the steps you take in order to achieve the goal. Being happy, that's the key; enjoying is everything.

CHAPTER 14

Whatever it Takes

We are guided by a desire, a passion, and the conviction of wanting something and loving a profession or sector. This desire is what makes us succeed, first of all as human beings, and then as professionals.

Life is full of situations and things that can happen, so knowing how we can adapt to them and how to direct all our efforts towards that end, that desire, that to which we aspire, will be the key to either winning our inner victory or failing to achieve it.

Getting something to fight for, live for, strive for or love can be the most difficult thing in life. Finding it allows the person to follow a passion, or, on the other hand, an excuse to pass the time; the time to live as we want. Because even if we don't think so, everyone, even people who are born with fewer opportunities, has a choice and the ability to decide where to go.

How do I know what I am passionate about?

We must find what makes us happy, so look at where you want to spend your working hours and where you want to spend your leisure time. Your working hours should not be considered an effort because it is not a job; it's something you love. If you can get to that level of feeling with something, there you will have the answer to the question.

If you are lucky enough to know what your passion is, then count yourself very fortunate because not many people have that or have the chance to experience it. Sometimes, things can be hard because nothing in this life is easy, and nothing is handed to you; however, you will have found a reason to live. The human being is what it is because of the desire to grow, to create, to improve and that is why passion and a taste for something makes us try harder for what we want. It is within all of us, so if you find that thing that makes you tick, something you really like, then go for it and don't look back; it will be the best thing you do in life.

Where does desire come from?

Desire comes from within and from the experiences we have had, how we adapt to life and what we choose to allow into our hearts and minds as happiness and enjoyment.

As we have seen in previous chapters, the most precious thing in life is "time". Today you are thirty years old and yesterday, it seems, you were only twenty; this is life; time flies. We must decide what we want to do with the time we have been given and know that each day, minute or second could be our last.

What we know is based on an accumulation of experiences and the lifestyle that we live day by day, thinking that we know everything that is wrong, but only once we begin to understand and know about life, we will begin to feel that we do not really know anything. Life is experiences and nobody is born knowing, but, without a doubt, we can be part of our learning process or not; it totally depends on us.

When you begin to understand what life is and you leave the comfort that your "home" gives you, that's when you start to really value things, when the little things become important, and when you start to get to know yourself and your ambitions better.

Effort and sacrifice should not be a part of your life, but of your DNA, but these two concepts should not be considered harsh; rather, the opposite. We talk about life and your work as a goal, an objective; but do we have something better to do?

Would we prefer to do nothing in life; just lie down all day? Life is not that and if you do not believe this, try it because you will not like it. We need targets, realistic ones but also ones that involve an effort that is worthwhile regarding your goals in life.

Working for what we want should be a habit, not something hard or unpleasant, because if it is, then you have not found what you were looking for.

The human being tends to want to be relaxed and not waste energy, and that is something that occurs naturally, but the mind, even if it tries to be calm, makes us want to create, discover and improve; that is why the human being dominates the world and the other animals on the planet. Therefore, the passion we feel and the desire to do things are something intrinsic that we have as human beings.

Therefore, do what you desire, what you really want to do; but forget about what other people say because is what you do that really matters. Be honest, respectful and smart when judging people, and no matter what happens, be happy.

In football, we must feel the same. If you want to be a professional footballer, there must be a mixture of desire and effort every day. It is essential to have a calm environment that allows you to work, and never listen to negative messages that make you doubt your potential. Stay positive, have good people around you and work hard. Jealousy of others is a normal thing to find in life. It is how we know how to adapt to all this; the key to being balanced enough in life to focus on your goal, on your passion.

We can share many targets in life; some people need many things to be happy, while other people don't need anything. We are just different, but what we all have in common is the "energy" to do things in life. Sometimes obstacles on our path try to change us as a person, but we need to fight against this. We need to be ourselves and not alter our objectives for any reason. Whatever it takes, we have to fight for us and our people, and not give up for any reason.

Extra comment/thought/feeling:
Mark Rivers
Currently working for Arsenal FC. Worked at the FA, Reading FC, Wimbledon, Plymouth Argyle FC, Wycombe Wanderers FC.

-About his passion for helping in the evolution and improvement of coaching in England, as well as the players and human beings around him, always whatever it takes-

Coaching for me comes down to understanding people and building relationships; understanding an individual's motivation. Motivation in transactional terms is different in everyone. Some will be motivated by money and power, whilst others have an intrinsic motivation for personal development and the evolution of others around them.

Personally, I believe I have an inner desire to help our young people to develop as people first but also to challenge them as players in order for them to reach their potential. It is important for me that I am consistent with my behaviours and values, and that I really take into consideration the brain development, maturation rates and any other external factors that may prohibit the player from maximising their productivity during our limited time together.

Checking in with ourselves, seeking regular feedback and listening to educate oneself and not to challenge are all ways that I try to enhance myself as a sports practitioner as I continue to strive to learn and progress throughout my personal journey.

The evolution of coaching has been astronomical in recent years, with practitioners who are serious about developing their craft continuing to strive for excellence. I believe that it is essential to value the individual and create a decision-rich environment to allow holistic learning to take place. Being able to recognise unconscious incompetence versus conscious competence, being age-specific with our approach to learning and supporting players, and an understanding that winning is a lovely by-product of development are all crucial elements in creating a platform that will allow the individual to thrive.

I try and create a culture that is built on respectful challenge, a culture that will stretch and challenge the coaching workforce, and a culture that will test the cognitive bandwidth of the coach to help strive for excellence. I believe that this is the grounding that is required to best support the end user.

CHAPTER 15

What You Need to Sacrifice

Most people live only to have fun and spend what they have, a lifetime, enjoying the pleasures that humans and nature have created for our comfort. But there is still a group of people who have other goals; apart from enjoying themselves, they want to leave something in the world once they die. They value the facts and what they can achieve in life, and I do not mean only material things, but things to do with honour. They have the dignity and strength to want to "be something in life", that desire to improve and fight that only a few understand and that affects the present and future of people. Surely there are some of you who are reading these words and know and understand what I mean.

We speak of a way of living and understanding life. Understand life as a fusion between passion and targets, where the path to achieving them is what marks your happiness and where pride in achieving goals is a fundamental strength. Have a goal and reach it, and most importantly, follow the path ahead of you, the plan, the effort and that value that is given to your own effort, pride, and personal honour to achieve it. Although it seems that these thoughts come from another time, it is not like that and there are still people who think and live this way.

Sacrificing your life would not be a good phrase to describe this pathway, because that is grounded in the thought of living with respect to some codes and leaving something in the world for the people who will come later; honour, pride, loyalty, principles, etc. These words are easy to say and difficult to follow day by day as the foundation of your personality as a human being. But the fundamental idea is to have a goal and achieve it with effort because all good things cost, and we all know that.

Morality enters the scene and makes us see this issue with greater perspective because it is part of our daily living and the decisions we make.

What are you willing to sacrifice to achieve that goal?

We are not talking about only physical effort; it can also be moral. Everything that comes from morality will affect you much more.

Would you be willing to betray a person to achieve your goals?

Questions like these may seem easy to answer, but they happen to all of us in a moment of time and it is in those moments that you will define yourself as a person.

Both in life and in football, there are corrupt situations where you will have to know how to move but never lose who you are, because if you go against your instincts, eventually, you will end up lost. Therefore, being you, but adapting to the situations will be the best way to carry on. And we all know our limits and the line that cannot be crossed.

Therefore, sacrifice implies the sacrifice of physical time but also of moral or personal factors, which I think are the most difficult to bear since they touch us directly inside.

How do I get a goal that allows me to live a life like this?

Look inside yourself and ask yourself what you want to do, what you are passionate about, and what gives meaning to your life. Then listen, speak, and argue with your people to find answers to the questions that come to you.

Each person is born in an environment that affects the level of goals and values. Each person is different, and we live in a world of experiences and contexts that affect what we feel and think every

What You Need to Sacrifice

day, week, month, and year. We are changing and evolving; we are not always the same. There are people who never find what they love or what they are predestined for, while others will never even want it and will want to live as comfortably as possible. Without a doubt, I believe that having goals and going for them will give meaning to your life, and that feeling of "fight" and desire is a feeling that cannot be explained; you simply have to feel it. However, once you do, I think most people are drawn to it as it makes you feel alive.

Even so, there will be periods of doubt where the target is not clear or because the path simply tires you mentally. You must strengthen your passion and your mind to endure and persevere on your way.

Football is a business where you have many ups and downs due to many circumstances, both as a player and in coaching or management positions. This happens because it is a very closed world, very popular and where the best and the worst are very close together. It is a business and a sport where there is a dilemma of loving it and hating it at the same time. "Love-Hate" - these are two words that sometimes go together in this sport. You love all of it because it is beautiful, pure, familiar, and agonistic; it is life on a playing field, yet, at the same time, it can be made rotten by many people who compose it, and sometimes anger and frustration can win over the love that is felt for it.

If the great feats of people have taught us anything, or, in this case, of football players, coaches, or managers, it is that nothing is given for free and if *you* don't fight, there will be another who is willing to do it and take you place. It is up to you whether or not you sacrifice your peace of mind to achieve your goal, but this is something that happens in all sectors at a high level. Competitiveness is at a maximum and only your mentality, patience and what you are willing to endure will be the difference between winning or losing.

If what you really want is football, remove all your fears, assume the difficulty, and plan; set your goals. Follow it and correct the things you must do along the way. Adapting is essential and keeping your targets and creating new ones is also healthy and important. Do not give up and do not lose your values, even if you adapt to the situation, as long as it does not cross the line of your morality. Learn from defeats and improve with victories as nobody knows everything and nobody is perfect. Be humble and never lose your identity despite the circumstances. Always have a Plan B, and the peace of mind that life is short, and you only live once.

There are very hard days physically and mentally, which undoubtedly make one wonder why you should make that effort, that sacrifice. But giving up should never be an option. Anyone can find excuses to give up; you can always find one. We should never do that.

Is the reward the goal? Is the achievement of the objective the only thing we must value? What should "the path" mean to us?

The achievement of the goal is undoubtedly important, and the key is not losing motivation, that inner energy of getting up every morning to fight for what you want. However, it shouldn't be the only thing that matters, and, in fact, it isn't. Life is time and experiences that you have, that which gives "meaning" to your history on earth, so the path is the ultimate goal that we will obtain and we will always have it with us in our memory. The path means the journey; it is life, experiences, and the time you live. The path means all the good and bad that we find ourselves in; it is the basis of life. The achievement of the targets must be valued, but even more so the path because the path is life and nothing has more value than life.

In football, apart from the titles and the nights of glory, what one misses are the teammates, the difficulties, and the collective effort of the team to improve, the talks, the anecdotes of the focus, the trips, to the things that shape you every day, your life as a footballer, the path of your life.

We also need to keep our dreams and protect them, because that's an amazing part of our life. Don't let anybody destroy them; do whatever it takes to find the way to be happy and even if you don't get all of them, you will feel proud and happy about your life.

As we said, a lot of people will not find any sense in these words, but we are talking about honour, so be proud of what you do and set goals rather than partying all day. For those of you who feel that these words are stupid and don't mean anything to you, take a seat and think about it twice, then let's find a purpose in life, try to help, to be useful to others; you can if you want to.

Give every effort to your goal in life because when you feel that it is the right reason, it's the meaning of your life. It is an amazing feeling that gives you hope, faith, and happiness. The sacrifice does not feel so big if you really love what you do, so find it, and enjoy the sacrifice.

Extra comment/thought/feeling:
Rodrigo Miño
Professional Economist and Lawyer.

We have always heard that motivation, sacrifice, and effort are key elements to successfully achieving targets in life. But...do we really know their meaning? Do we know how to apply them in our life project?

Below, I have tried to explain some tips which, in some way, could help anybody from a practical viewpoint. However, the real learning depends on each person and their attitude towards the targets we want to reach.

Everything starts with setting goals. Setting goals in any area of our lives allows us to set up a horizon towards which we must untiringly strive, and which constitutes a real motivation. However, an objective can be achieved in different ways and each of those ways constitutes a path that will determine us as human beings. In the same way that there are no bad or good people but actions that make us bad or good, the path we choose to achieve a goal will greatly shape the kind of person we will transform ourselves into. Therefore, for the setting of objectives, we must consider not only the what but the how. And it is at this point that the idea of effort and sacrifice appears.

The achievement of ambitious goals in life is very rarely attained in a fleeting way and without any investment. Choosing the fast path often involves assuming costs (personal and/or professional) which do not offset the final output. Think of a person who has achieved financial independence carrying out fraud and deceitful actions. This person will have achieved their target but without the conviction of a real effort and sacrifice which must be considered as their own.

Moreover, our goals require constant effort and sacrifice which implies an opportunity cost that we must consider in advance. By choosing a goal, and implementing certain actions, we give up other issues under the premise that the materialization of that goal will compensate for what we have left behind. Likewise, we not only assume an opportunity cost but also an uncertainty in case we do not reach the set objective. Think, for example, of those people who decide to apply for a new position and, for this purpose, they spend all their time studying and move away from their social relationships. These people may finally pass and obtain a permanent post for their entire life or, on the contrary, fail. But even in failure, people learn and know themselves better than even those who have not tried it.

Setting goals and achieving them is hard work which requires effort, dedication, and sacrifice. Therefore, we must move away from easy solutions, as nobody is going to give us anything without an investment on our part. The most important thing in life is the practical application of an unavoidable attitude aimed at the best possible endeavour for oneself.

Applying this, we can know from a logical point of view the importance that everything that matters in life has a cost but also a benefit at the end of the path. Sacrifice and motivation are two sides of the same coin which require active management.

CHAPTER 16

Spiritual Suicide

Everything in life depends on the mind, and consequently, on what we feel - happiness or misfortune. Knowing how to control our emotions is difficult and each one of us faces problems or experiences in life in different ways. Happiness is not a continuous state of mind, but it comes at times and depends on many factors. The normal thing is that we are in a constant calm situation in our lives, with better moments and worse ones. Unhappiness is the same, but it can become chronic and lead to psychological problems.

We must try to make our life belong to ourselves, which means understanding what we want, interpreting our situation and knowing how to carry it out. Even with that, our life goes through so many changes that one will never fully know if we are going on the right path or not, but these doubts will be part of our whole life forever and it is the same for everyone, even in a short period of time.

Life is like friendship, and we have to water it day by day, week by week and we must be in control of going where we want because it is the only thing we can choose; the same applies to almost all of us. We have decision-making power and many times we do not use it because of fears; fears that come from society or from people who tell us that it is impossible, or that we are crazy. The reality is that we can change our life, but we need the desire to do it, and first admit to ourselves what we are doing wrong in order to have the mindset to change and improve.

Spiritual Suicide

Get up in the morning and feel that you are doing what you like or that you are at least fighting for an end, or even doing what you do for people that you care about, such as your children or family or simply to maintain the stability of your family. That gives you a target. Living without targets and, above all, fighting for goals you don't believe in, is losing you life, selling your time for nothing, and dying alive.

The goal should be that when it is time to die, you look up at the ceiling and feel that your life made sense and you achieved what you wanted. If that moment comes and you don't feel that, you may have wasted your life and remember that you only live once. This is not a rehearsal.

Regretting what you didn't do is the worst feeling in the world. Just live and do not be afraid; fear is a barrier that you build on your own. Often, we think that people are thinking bad things about us or that they are looking at us, etc. Even if they are, it doesn't matter because, in a relatively short time, we will all die, so focus on what is important and on the important things in life, not on nonsense and false fears.

The world of football is tough and many times the pressure will make you wonder if pursuing this goal is the right thing to do. The dilemma of loving and hating football at the same time is a feeling that many professionals have. But we must understand that in all professions, at the highest level, we are always going to find things that we do not like. Corruption is found at all levels and professions of society, and we must adapt or withdraw. Another option may be to try to change the business, but it will have to be done from within, so adaptation is key in this process.

In a love/hate scenario, love always wins while hate keeps us alert but never makes us withdraw unless we reach the limit.

There are many examples of mistakes that we can make that we could call "spiritual suicide". I have listed a few below – see if you identify with any of them.

The Things We Know and Do Not Say

When you live where others want you to
When you live how others want you to
When you study what others want you to
When you say something but do the opposite
When you love something and do not pursue it
When you deceive yourself or others
When you hurt those who love you most
When you feel sorry and do nothing to remedy it
When you do not feel anything
When you let love escape out of fear
When you interpret life as a business
When you don't have any goals in life
When you interpret your life just as goals and you don't have a social life
When you put aside what you really want for material things
When material things possess you and not vice versa
When you sacrifice your time for trivial things that do not make you grow as a person

    No one knows what rules this world, or what will happen tomorrow or in a hundred years from now, or if there is something after death or if there is a god or if it is just our imagination. Yet, what we do every day is the most important thing. Knowing that there are opportunities every day to get a little happiness allows you to look to tomorrow with energy and new expectations.

    To laugh or cry? Sometimes we don't know what to do because we don't find our path in this world, but we should know that this is a completely normal thing that happens to everybody. How you deal with yourself in those moments of pain is the key to keep working and growing as a person. As we said before, having goals is also a good ally to success because with no goals there is no motivation, and that will always end badly.

    What will lead us to wake up every morning?

It is my honest belief that we have this answer inside, and it will be different for all of us, but if you find it, you will be happy, free and your spirit will be a "winner". Do not be ashamed to fail or fall in life; just be ashamed of people, or even yourself, if you don't try to have a "real" life. The one who fails at least tried it, and we must value when people are trying with everything they have.

Ask the right questions, find the answers and work for it, then you will get what you were looking for. We are not talking about achieving great things, or even what people think about you, we are just talking about YOU, and that is the most important thing in this life - your own view and happiness.

Do not lose faith in what you feel and desire because that is all we have in this world; surround yourself with good people and follow what you see, touch and taste; do not follow the ideas or dreams of others; follow what you can see, real things, and then mix them with your dreams then you will have a nice path to follow and share with the people you care about.

If you feel that you are wasting your time, or that your life doesn't make sense for whatever reason, stop, and think about what you want to do, then plan and go for it. We just have one life. Often, we don't realize that sooner or later we will die, maybe even tomorrow, and we can't take material things there. So, we need to enjoy life for life itself, and if not, change something in order to get what we desire.

Extra comment/thought/feeling:
We must have the courage to "live" and forget about fears, as fear is a barrier that we put on ourselves.

CHAPTER 17

Health

Health comes first because, without health, nothing exists.

But what do we call health today?

Today, our jobs are not as physical as in the past, so the mind works more than before, but it is also more exposed; exposed to many marketing messages, electronic elements, and advertisements; also, with an education based on theory rather than making people think and work things out, so we are getting worse, and people are not trained to realize it. In short, mental health is in danger and we are not prepared for it. The new generations are increasingly wealthy and weak. It is difficult to think that without the right help, many people will be able to maintain a healthy and balanced life.

How to achieve proper health: That is the question, and it is what we must work on, but above all, we must know what is good for us on a physical, mental and social level. A balanced life between the three is the key. Do not favour one over the other, as balance is always the key in life.

In football, as in any sport, an athlete must give importance to the balance between the three fundamentals which are training, food, and rest. Because if you train a lot but don't eat well and rest, it will be useless, and the same can be said for the other two. On a mental level, a football player finds himself/herself at a more difficult level than other sports, because of the repercussions that football has on society and what this generates in the person and his/her life. You can earn more money which allows you to have a life with more comforts, but, at the same time, it generates personal stress as an individual in a society that knows you, so the life you can lead is not normal. The greater the fame, the more difficulty there will be, although it is compensated by more material possessions, but this can never supply us with what we value as freedom.

For a footballer, going back to his/her childhood, close circle of friends, the people who love him/her and those memories as a young man/woman when he/she was not known will be the key to maintaining that emotional balance. Discover who you are, know yourself, do not forget about your soul and, above all, improve but never change within yourself; change what the environment changes.

And it is precisely this fact that is important to highlight. Situations, circumstances and even people can change but never your inside goals and the values that give you that balance and stability.

As we have said, it is the balance between the physical, mental, and social levels that will make us succeed. Those are the principal things to take care of in order to have good health, and they do not work on their own but each one has an influence on the other.

Bodily health is really important these days where we live in cities, where our work leads us to live a stressful and competitive life and also where we don't eat proper healthy food. "Mens sana in corpore sano" – "A sound mind in a healthy body" is the sentence that defines that our body needs to be fit because the relations with the brain, with your emotions and with your feelings are so strong.

We have many options to improve our health, but we should focus on a healthy diet and physical exercise. To eat healthily, begin by having between four and five meals per day, but the most important is what we eat and how. We have to partner this with proper physical exercise and have a routine that fits with our work and other duties. What we know for sure is that being fit helps us to have a healthy mind, and for this, we need to focus on a good diet and routines that help us to be consistent.

The human body needs to move, and just walking can help to maintain healthy progress. We have many other actions in our daily routine that are not proper exercises but which could help us, like climbing the stairs, walking or dancing. We know that physical inactivity is one of the factors of premature death and can also provoke certain diseases, so fighting against sedentarism is one of the challenges of the next few decades. This will aid the battle against cardiovascular problems, stress, pressure, diabetes and high cholesterol and improve physical stability and flexibility. We must focus on increasing the cardio levels, working the strength, facilitating the mobility of the whole body and attaining a proper weight.

As a football player, I do not have problems with exercising, but knowing what I am doing, how to improve my health and above all, how to achieve maximum performance, is important, and nobody explains it to us. Training a lot is useful but it must be done at specific times, with a designated meal plan and breaks, otherwise, we will be wasting time; organization is the key to success.

Secondly, we must talk about mental health which goes together with physical health. Playing sport, going to the gym, or even just walking helps us to feel better, although sport gives you a way of meditating to fight depression and bad feelings, putting you in a good position to feel confident and getting the endorphins surging.

Poor mental health is a problem that has been at the forefront for years and we already know many ways to combat it, however, it is vital that we look for what makes us happy and pursue it. And above all, we must appreciate what we have because there are many people in the world who do not have our opportunities. Travelling can be a good way to know what we have and to appreciate the size of the world we live in. Appreciating what we have is key to improving as a human being, and being better for yourself and for the people around you.

Be aware of what we can contribute to the community through the chances we have that many others don't get as that can lead us to better all round. It's because of these facts that we improve as humans. We need to be aware of what we have, because, as we said before, in a hundred years we will all be dead and we need to be happy and enjoy this life now. Sometimes the little things are the most important, like just saying sorry, or I love you – the smallest things can change everything.

As a professional footballer, you can suffer from depression caused by many factors; because of all the attention you have, stress, even when you retire and see that you have lived in a "bubble" and not as many people care about you as before. Taking care of what we think and feel is key, so keep your feet on the ground and always know who you are and what you are, no more, no less.

The third and last part of this chapter is social health: We are humans, and we need to socialize in order to feel alive. This is a human need to be with other people and to feel part of a team, a family or a group. The human being is a social being, and we need the affection of others, laughter, communication, discussion and sharing feelings just to feel alive.

We must always try to maintain a balance between responsibilities and social life as having friends, going out and sharing your life with others helps to improve your self-satisfaction and the perception of life that you have as much in yourself as in your environment.

As football players, your list of "friends" will grow, but it is there where you should identify who is with you for what you do, and who is there for who you are, for the person. It is so important not to trust everyone, nor to distrust everyone, but to know how to look inside people is a great virtue. However, you can at least count on your own circle, those who have always been and will be forever, your family and real friends.

Moreover, we should know that when we are happy, we make others happy; we send positive feelings to people and these things improve the world. We are all in the same "boat" helping each other, even if we are not aware of it.

Extra comment/thought/feeling:
Happiness is in you, not in material things; everyone has things, but not everyone is really happy.

CHAPTER 18

Routines

All living beings have duties and tasks to perform with a clear objective of survival. Routine has a lot to do with the order and patterns that human beings have created to organize these daily tasks and is something that simply defines a way of life that we repeat many times, over a long period of time. It also gives us a feeling of control over what we do, bringing us security and peace of mind in our lives.

Organization is the foundation of all success, even for people who don't like effort. Good organization/routine means you will not waste time and allows you to take advantage of all the time you want to have available for your goal. A person with good and orderly routines is an intelligent person because he/she works with objectives and, above all, with a plan.

There are two ways to feel about what a routine does to us. On the bad side, it is hard and sometimes very tiring, implying a part of life that we don't like, which is "always doing the same thing", which many people try to avoid because they don't like it. There is also a good side which is that routine can create models and organizational structures for daily, weekly or specific objectives, which keep you focused and with your mind concentrated on achieving the objective following that model created before you began.

For a footballer, it is very important to have routines.
Why?

When you are a professional footballer, or any other profession in the world, if you really want to be good, you have to adopt some habits and follow patterns of behaviour and daily work that allow you to have a level, improve it and maintain it over time. This is only possible with the creation of routines that allow you to know what to do, and that give you the peace of mind that you need for it. Without order, chaos comes, and this does not help; it only takes away your chances of success. It is difficult to get there but even more difficult to maintain a high level of performance, so, for this reason, routine is key because it makes you stay focused and perform.

What we must take into account are the limits, because there are always limits in everything in life.

When can routine turn into obsession or illness?

Routine should help, but we must be careful not to cause an emotional imbalance caused by overexertion at work or in the imposing of the routine itself. Everything is good until you go overboard and cross those limits. The limits can be identified from the experience of others in the past or you can discover new ones yourself. As we saw in previous chapters, having a balance is the key to avoid falling into negativity and ruin at all levels.

In the end, it is always the balance between all things which makes the human being have the base and foundations to achieve their goals from there. Routine is good for organizing and controlling your daily effort but it also "gets old" and generates exhaustion from boredom. Most importantly, we must consider different options in our week that may help us stay motivated.

For a football player, having a routine that gives you habits in terms of hours of sleep, meals, training, and study is the key to reaching the elite and, above all, staying motivated, which is usually difficult. We need to do our work and have "getaways" that clear the mind such as breaks, social activities, time with friends, etc. Those reinforce the socio-emotional and cognitive part of the player that we are.

PLANNING – ORGANIZATION – CONTROL

Routine brings comfort but can easily induce complacency, that is why it should be controlled and never exceed certain limits because then it would lose its purpose. We talk about the mind; that, for the human being, is everything, because we are capable of the best and the worst depending on how our mind works. We must learn to be well, to be happy and to guide our efforts to clear and planned objectives.

We are living in a competitive world where you must prove every day who you are; that's not fair but it's what it is so we have to be ready for it. Have a plan, a routine, to help you to become more committed to carrying out tasks and making things easier day by day.

A routine is a process whereby you organise your time to be consistent in performing daily tasks. How do we know which is the best routine for us? We must focus on 3 words:

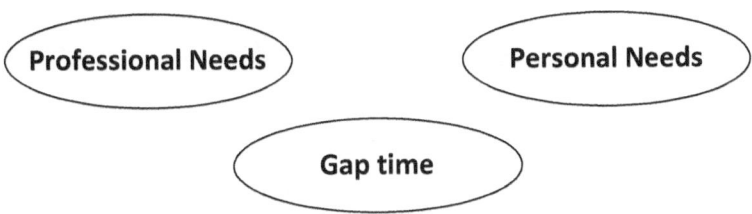

Your professional needs are always, or almost always, the priority because it is what feeds us. The coordination of these with our personal needs will grow in importance as we grow. Finally, we always need gap time where we can have room to rest or save free time since unforeseen events can always occur.

POSITIVES
Monitoring your own time
Organise/coordinate your work and personal time better
Control your emotions

NEGATIVES
It is tiring
Less motivated

To combat the negative things, we should make changes some days, as sometimes it's important to let the brain relax and be flexible. A routine is good and bad at the same time, so being successful depends on how much importance we give to our personal needs in order to do the routine properly but also being motivated to do it.

Now we have to talk about whether the routine is good or bad for us in terms of lifestyle. Routine is the antagonist of "chaos", so we could tell that routine is a good thing, but we have to think further and be aware of why this world is always controlled by routines and timetables. Routine is good but too much routine makes life miserable and boring and does not let us be open-minded and flexible in what we do. We need to realise that we need routine to help us to do our duties, but, at the same time, we need an "open" life where you don't plan every single thing. Governments like to control their citizens so they will always promote routines, plans, work, and everything else to pay their taxes and have the people under control. We need to go further and live a normal and structured life but also be aware of these things and enjoy the "chaos" sometimes by being flexible and adaptable.

In this world, we already have a routine imposed; for example, with the days of the week. What do the days of the week represent, or what do Mondays represent?

In today's world, Monday represents the day we start again; the first day of the week. Someone said that we had to work a series of days and start again on Monday, so we wake up and we do it. That is why no one is very happy on Mondays.

We have invented Mondays as a way to control the work we do. Someone invented that day to define it as the first workday of the week. Without a doubt, it is something that has been established throughout the world, and it is partly good because, without order, the world could not exist; the chaos of disorder would destroy everything. As we have said, it is order or routine that leads us to great things, controlling the limits, and, above all, accepting that life is based on an orderly and planned system, which helps everything make sense, but at the same time, we are controlled by it. It is in ourselves as individuals not to allow ourselves to be controlled and to live according to what we believe and love. We must use these tools that we know to achieve our goals and, at the same time, to be happy in our free time that we have pre-organised within the set routine.

Routine, yes, but with its limits, always measuring what causes us stress and adjusting it for our good. Remember that each person is different and that each of us has our needs, so, what for one person could be a good routine, for another person it may not. The self-awareness of our own limitations is key.

Extra comment/thought/feeling:
Pablo Borges
PHD Sport Sciences. Professor at University of La Laguna (Spain). Former Club Atlético de Madrid, Getafe CF, CD Leganés FC, Rayo Vallecano.

What does it depend on if you can reach your best version? Surely, on many things that you know well enough, and others that you just have to discover step by step. To do this, I suggest you start by carrying out a SETTING OF OBJECTIVES. The reason for this is that to achieve something in our life, whether in sports or in studies, we must be very clear about WHERE we want to go and WHAT we want to achieve, but above all, and this is the most important thing, HOW we are going to achieve it.

Why is this so important? Because having objectives has a very positive influence on practically everything that affects performance and in many other areas (studies, family, etc.). The objectives will help us to be focused on what we must do, as if it were a very useful manual. It can stimulate energy and effort, but it will also help to maintain it and persist in it, creating strategies, and keeping attention on the reasons why we are doing it. For this reason, self-confidence, and confidence to be able to perform at the highest level are important, and in order to do this, it is necessary to control expectations through the SMART objectives:

- Specific: They must be as specific as possible (concrete actions).
- Measurable: That they can be counted in some way (to check if we have achieved them or not).
- Achievable: Our challenges should be difficult but, at the same time, reachable.
- Realistic: Go step by step and work hard to achieve it, but always be realistic.
- Time-bound: An "expiration" date, short, medium and long-term goals.

Once we are clear about the objectives that you set for yourself, and especially taking into account the situation we are experiencing (forced confinement due to the coronavirus), where we began to value other insignificant things weeks ago, such as going out on the streets, walking, seeing a friend, etc., we realize that important things are not material; they cannot be touched, they cannot be bought, they are simply enjoyed.

For this reason, I propose that you create a routine, which is defined by the DRAE as "A custom or acquired habit of doing something in a certain way, which does not require having to reflect or decide." Routines will help us to do things in a simpler and more comfortable way and, above all, to maintain this behaviour over time. That is why it begins with those things that have to do with you - your health, with the importance of maintaining certain habits, such as a stable sleep schedule and/or adequate nutrition, which will allow your body to synchronize with its biological rhythm.

Establish, if you need to, a schedule from Monday to Friday and another for the weekend. In this way, you can exercise greater control over what you want to do at all times and achieve a normalization of the day-to-day events. Actively occupy your free time; spend time studying, spend time with family and friends or learn something new, but don't forget to spend some time with yourself, reflecting on what you have done during the day and planning what you will do the next day.

For example, several studies (Martínez, 2017) have shown that being an active person helps improve memory and our mood, as well as helping to reduce stress by releasing neurotransmitters such as dopamine, related to pleasure and associated with the sensation of relaxation, serotonin, related to happiness, regulation of appetite, sleep and mood, and endorphins, which regulate anxiety and intervene in the feeling of well-being.

"The essential is invisible to the eyes" (The Little Prince).

CHAPTER 19

Self-Confidence and Trust

Throughout the book, we are going to talk about self-confidence because it is one of the pillars on which our personality must be based in order to live a full life and be able to achieve our goals. There is a phrase that is always repeated - we cannot transmit confidence or trust if we first don't have confidence in ourselves. This basically means that firstly, we must trust ourselves, and from there, transmit those good vibrations and trust in others. We live in a world of social relationships, where synergies are fundamental, and within these synergies, we are part of the equation, and our way of acting and being with ourselves and others is key. We often achieve many things in life just by believing that we are better than what we really are, or just by being fully aware of who we are and not belittling our talent to anything or anyone.

What do I think of myself?

What we think about ourselves, what we feel when we look in the mirror, that confidence or lack of it in ourselves is what we transmit to others, and it plays a fundamental part in the way that people think about us. Knowing ourselves and wanting to improve day by day is key because our actions are what will make us have a better self-concept and attain that confidence that makes us achieve our goals.

Self-confidence is the pillar to being able to set big goals, because, on the way to success, we have to face situations, problems with people, with a multitude of things that we only know how to control and overcome with confidence in ourselves. Without confidence, our self-esteem will be low, and that is what we will also transmit to others, who will tend not to believe in us and what we say. Everything is linked and interrelated.

The confidence that a person has is related to their deepest fears, which are born from complexes and bad experiences. Knowing how to face what we fear is key to improving, because life will never be easy; we will always see things that have to be overcome. Confidence can be worked on and improved. We can get to control what we feel and how things affect us, improve our self-concept, and become stronger in all areas. Everything in life requires work, self-confidence, and trust as well.

It all starts from the wisdom of knowing, understanding and being sure of the talent we have, and always being humble and realistic about our abilities, never arrogant. Confidence in achieving goals is important, as is how we see ourselves achieving those goals. However, this depends on our past experience or the perception that we may have of our worth at a more general level. Although confidence does play this important part, we must be honest with ourselves, especially when getting a clear conception of reality regarding successes and failures. This is based on honesty, understanding that we cannot control everything that happens and, at the same time, feeling good about our possibilities and avoiding the fears that put a barrier between us and our goals.

Trust is based on the basic principle of socialization that human beings have. The human being is a social being; we can be alone but not always alone. The communication skills and characteristics that we have acquired over time enable us to be sociable and procreate, which is the fundamental principle of why there are women and men. Therefore, we are designed to be sociable.

To be sociable, do you need to trust that person?

These topics can be related, directly or indirectly, because although socially you do not need to know the person completely, you need at least to have the certainty and security that the person with whom you communicate is going to return the greeting and he/she is not going to hurt you. That establishes a relationship, although sometimes it is minimal. Even when we walk down the street, for example, we adapt to others, we look and trust that the people around us will not push us into the road; trusting relationships occur all the time.

In life, we are born with our mother, then the father comes and then you meet the rest of the family. In the beginning, the relationship of trust with your parents is the greatest you have, and from there, it is the facts, circumstances and contexts that determine which ones become your trusted people. Throughout life, many things will happen, good and bad. For example, some friends will always stay the same but others will change due to circumstances such as changes in country, work, etc. It is normal and should not affect who you are as a person.

The normal thing is that your trust in others is reduced as life passes because we all find ourselves in negative situations that cause us fear or suspicion against other people or situations. The reality is that there are many good people in the world, but also many bad people, so we need to be aware of it.

Experience will help us to moderate our way of meeting people and letting them enter our world, but it will also cause us to be insecure about the people around us if those experiences were negative. The key is a balance as not everyone is good but not everyone is bad either. Therefore, a balance on how open you are is crucial here.

In football, trust must be earned. Football is like a cake, and each person wants their part of it. There are many people who will sell other people, even friends, to gain a foothold in the industry. You have to know it and get to know the environment, which will take time,

Self-Confidence and Trust

so, in the beginning, be very careful with all those who approach you; the interest of people will grow or decrease according to your achievements. This is the current situation and it will never change.

Be smart enough to surround yourself well, learn from mistakes and above all, do not talk more than you should. You only own what you keep to yourself, so if you tell people about it, everyone will know. Talking more than necessary will always cause you problems, so focus on your life and work and listen, but keep what you think to yourself. Share it only with your people, with that small group of three or four friends who are with you in the good and the bad moments; otherwise, it will be very difficult for you to survive in the business because whatever you say could be used against you, even if they are lies. Still, you must remember that it was you who gave them the weapons to attack you, so you caused it to happen. If you don't speak up, you will never allow anyone to use anything against you.

Obviously, there will be a group of people in your life to whom you can express yourself freely and where you are not judged or misunderstood; this is where you can be as open as you want. On the other hand, being open-minded has nothing to do with what we have been talking about. Being open-minded is good and it is the way it should be, to be able to speak frankly, with serenity and from the heart, from your most intimate thoughts.

Trust also creates ties and synergies. These synergies are the basis of life since we live in an open and moving environment where we all exert something on other people. Not trusting anyone will make you lose all these options and possibilities that others offer you. Trying to be open and maintain a balance between those we trust or not is difficult, but we must be patient and accept the blows as a boxer receives them and keep fighting until the end.

What we do in life and the values we have, define us as human beings. It's not the money or the recognition; it's just how we are. We are born and we have parents, teachers, and friends who teach us how to do everything; your personality and values grow at the same time and provide you with the opportunity to show who you are. There are many types of people, but to be a person in whom people can trust, you need to have values and there are not many people with good values at the moment.

What you feel for people and what you do will also define how people can trust you. The reality is that whether you are a great person or a loser, the context is the same – we are what we do. To want, to achieve, to desire; these are verbs that mean the same, and imply effort, trust, and passion. They are also words that describe how to get the most out of life. For example, sacrificing your time for someone or for a cause defines what you want, and what you desire, and you must be carried away by those feelings, that passion; it's the "natural instinct" that will make you feel great and will change your life because, at that moment, you will feel alive and nothing else will matter to you apart from it.

It is precious to trust and we are lucky when we find people in the world who, although they are not family, are trusted friends. But remember, we cannot trust everybody, even your parents, if they don't show you "love". When someone loves you, they show it with actions, not just telling you. When we love somebody, we would do anything for that person, and, no matter what, we are there for him/her. You will have a lot of people around telling you that they love you, but that's not love, it's just a ruse to get you to trust them. Analyse those people, what they give to you, how they help for nothing, and from there, you will find out who is truly your friend, judging by their actions in good times and especially in bad times.

We should be careful about people, and, when you are successful in your career, you should be even more careful, because you will find a lot of people who were never there, telling you how good you are. We cannot trust somebody that tells us good things when he/she doesn't know us; only trust the people who truly know you and who talk to you face to face, telling you both the good and the bad things; those people are the trusted ones.

In summary, being open-minded is good, but being open with everyone is not, so keep your thoughts private and don't let many people in. Never forget that apart from your parents and a few good and trusted friends, it can be very hard to find good people – sad, but true in the real world today.

Extra comment/thought/feeling:
Julio Martínez García
Professional football physical coach. Former Club Atlético de Madrid and Football Clubs at First Division in México, Honduras and Perú.

Despite the threat of a severe storm, that Sunday, with a dark and turbulent dawn that denied the usual hot Honduran sunrise, it seemed that even the last of the living conspired so that in a miraculous way, the sky would open at the precise time to coincide with the fanatical followers of the two main teams in the country, that on September 12, 2004, on the highly anticipated seventh date of the Apertura Tournament, they finally faced each other in a classic that paralyzed everything.

Our Manager, Carlos D. Jurado, who liked to promote young values, made to debut a player named E. Izaguirre, who would later develop the most successful part of his career at Celtic F.C. in Glasgow. He is still playing professionally back at his original club, F.C. Motagua, where I had the satisfaction of working during my early experience in Central America.

From his official debut, E. Izaguirre had played every minute in front of thousands of people who usually filled the National Stadium of Tegucigalpa, offering a great performance that was improving noticeably. The atmosphere of mounting pressure during the week leading up to the match was shown on the faces of some players. That young man, who had very high self-confidence, which had deservedly led him to earn the greatest professional opportunity of his short football career, was already away from the team's hotel with visible signs of restlessness, despite his enormous and useless effort to hide it.

That Sunday evening, during the warm-up before a fiery and deafening crowd, despite my attempts to help him with words, phrases, gestures and encouragement, motivation and support, his fear and nervousness were increasingly evident. Back in the locker room, while each player finalized their preparations and carried out their particular and individual rituals, I continued without taking my eyes off him, and I seemed to see him turn increasingly pale and disfigured. Moments later, in the dark exit tunnel, before descending a long staircase that led to the field of play, I could see how his legs trembled like elongated jellies encased in stockings and boots, while he sweated adrenaline. Suddenly, as if evaporated, there was not a trace left of that boy full of self-confidence that I had met four months before, as, at that moment, he looked to be on the edge of death.

The game began, and as is easy to imagine, for that struggling footballer, everything went wrong. His first control, his first pass, his first duel, everything failed; Furthermore, he also fouled on our first throw-in, while his state of anxiety grew without signs of ending. After 35 minutes of running out of his mind, fleeing from his own ghosts and fears, he began to have cramps, asked for a change and finally, with no other choice, despite the reluctance of the coach, had to be replaced as he was completely broken and exhausted.

How was it possible that that same player in top form, who had come from playing the previous six games, travelling kilometres without rest until the last minute of the game, in just over half an hour was "dead"?

Self-Confidence and Trust

That was the first time that I saw with such clarity and evidence the devastating effect that fear has when it seizes us and our confidence vanishes, leaving us completely helpless and abandoned.

Nobody is aware that a high level of stress not only greatly affects the technical ability of the player, but also blocks him mentally, and the physical exhaustion caused by such a torrent of hormones can even be disabling. That day, I realized how suddenly you can lose the confidence that is so difficult to build. There, I could clearly see that without confidence, there is no performance, and without mutual trust, there is no team.

If one stops to reflect on the importance of confidence and trust in a person's life, it is easy to deduce that they play a cardinal role. The problem is that we may not ask ourselves sufficiently what exactly confidence and trust mean, what confidence and trust are, or how they are built and maintained. What is obvious is the determining role that they play in our personal and professional development, being the foundations of any human relationship, and a key and unfailing element for the successful completion of whatever we want to undertake in life. Every day, we can listen to television and radio commentators saying that a player is fine because he has great confidence, or that he needs the trust that the coach does not give him, etc. In the simplest gestures of body language, trust or mistrust in others and in situations are easy to observe.

We also constantly hear in press conferences or in statements to the media, references to trust when a coach states that he fully trusts his team, or in the work done during the week or during the season, or of course, even in the trust that one has in divine providence and in the saints, or in a family member who may rest in peace who will lend us a hand from another world to get us out of a meeting in good standing, which, although not widely acknowledged, still happens, such as wearing the same shirt with which the last game was won, or carrying a figure of the Virgin in one's pocket, etc.

As we can deduce from all this, there are different types of confidence and trust, and of course, their construction and development are something very complex and multifactorial, taking their role from genetics, the social environment in which we live, or the way we have been educated by our parents and our closest environment with their reinforcements and punishments. There are those who seem to have a lot of confidence and show it with an enviable natural flair, and then, on the other hand, there are those who face the effort of the fight every day to find even a tiny piece of it and keep it. Of course, it is something that everyone needs, and I suppose that each person tries, in his own way, and with the tools he has, to acquire confidence, because it is always more pleasant and reassuring to undertake objectives with confidence in yourself and trust in those around you.

When we watch a tennis match, it is interesting to see a player who was inspired five minutes ago and scored points easily, playing his best tennis, but suddenly, when he misses two or three shots, that confidence is changed into insecurity and is capable of altering the whole game. It is especially here, in the more technical sports, when self-confidence becomes more important when striving to reach the maximum potential of an athlete. Disputing a match point, playing the last basketball shot or taking the decisive penalty in the final of a title, are not actions that are explained and resolved only with arguments of sports technique or physical condition, but require self-confidence as an element integral to all of them and, from my point of view, superior to everything else.

People who hate to compete try to get as far away as possible from situations that make them put themselves to the test. However, no matter how much they do this, they have no choice but to accept that living involves overcoming challenges daily, in infinite ways that require self-confidence to a greater or lesser extent. Yet, when a person ends up voluntarily practising a certain sport or activity that leads

Self-Confidence and Trust

him/her to confront others, or himself/herself, it is because at least to some degree, it stimulates, attracts, or even loves competition. All the attributes necessary to achieve our dreams, achieve our goals and achieve success, go through confidence and trust, that intangible and sometimes ignored muscle which needs, probably more than the rest, permanent training, attention, and daily care for most of us. And I don't think that confidence and trust are underrated qualities, but are largely left neglected without being given the necessary attention.

Competition, the need for good results, and both the fear of failure and achievement are, for most people, very stressful, and even more so among those who are more inclined towards competition and challenges. Suffering from precompetitive stress is something typical and more common than we might suppose, and I would even dare to say that in a way, it is also taboo. However, it is precisely confidence, i.e., security in oneself and in our abilities, that makes these levels of stress controlled, leading the subject to be truly inspired by their activity or with little conviction and result in the realization of a task. This is called the Arousal level, which is the level of stress or arousal that is above or below a certain threshold, where performance decreases. Therefore, said level of activation or stress, of restlessness or nervousness, must be within adequate margins. That is why it will be difficult for both an excessively relaxed or too nervous player to have an optimal performance.

We constantly see how teams of a superior category, compared to other much humbler ones, are surprisingly and painfully defeated or eliminated from a certain competition precisely because of that excess of confidence that leads them to face a match without concentration or intensity. Personally, I have "panic" for those typical games that you have to play against the bottom of the league, or against a team of the lower category precisely because the footballer feels much more relaxed and unthreatened, and it involves a great effort as coaches to make sure this does not happen during the previous training days;

while on the opposite side, the motivation when you have to face a great team in a magnificent stadium is given by itself and it is enough to hinder the generation of enthusiasm that is spontaneously created, so that the group responds for itself at its full potential, regardless, of course, of the final score.

One of the desirable products of confidence is that of an always purposeful attitude to mistakes or discouragement. If there is something also shared by people who usually enjoy great self-confidence, it is their relationship with error. All successful people improve when they fail, because thanks to their confidence, they are able to persist in turning error into learning, and not collapsing or abandoning anything, because they are nonconformists aware of their capabilities that are not usually intimidated by the fear of failure, and they want to continue tirelessly improving and perfecting themselves.

There are two key elements which are substantially different, subordinating one to the other in their coexistence, and these are self-esteem and self-concept. For both, a certain level of self-knowledge is essential, which leads us to know what our strengths and weaknesses are, how far the strengths of our abilities go and where the limits of our abilities lie, to try as much as possible, reduce the distance between our ideal self and our real self. This is of vital importance when it comes to being objective in setting possible and achievable goals, or unattainable things that make us frustrated in our existence.

Fundamentally, while self-concept is the image we have of ourselves, self-esteem is the subjective emotional assessment of that image. Depending on the self-concept we have of ourselves, our self-esteem will be higher or lower.

Self-esteem is simply the feeling of appreciation or self-love that a person has towards himself/herself and his/her global assessment, the basis of a healthy personality that allows him/her to develop his/her full potential by facing failures with acceptance and adaptability,

Self-Confidence and Trust

and whose foundations were obviously beginning to be established in childhood as a necessary element for emotional and effective stability in order to achieve the desired state of balance and reasonable well-being and happiness.

However, self-concept has a more cognitive character, and becomes the mental representation that we establish through the set of thoughts and ideas we have about ourselves, our virtues, talents, qualities and personal traits, giving us a clearer answer to the question, "Who am I?"

Achieving a level of self-esteem consistent with our way of being undoubtedly contributes to harmony in our relationships with others, and these relationships, in turn, in order to be healthy and constructive, must be based on trust in the other.

In this dimension, trust is, of course, an act that carries its dangers. We can always be fooled by others. I, who already feel that I am on the Thursday of my life, have met many people who live in a permanent state of mistrust towards everything and everyone. And frankly, I don't know how you can live like this, because there is no manifestation in life that does not require at least surrender to the possibility of disappointment, betrayal, or deception. We need to trust our manager, our doctor, our lawyer, the school where we take our children, or the restaurant we go to, for example. When we buy something online, we trust that we are acquiring what we truly think it is and not something of worse quality, and this is the case with absolutely everything. We always need to trust.

When a coach calls me and invites me to join his coaching staff, he is placing all his trust in me, something that flatters me to the same extent that he makes me responsible, because he is putting a huge and decisive part of his personal project in my hands, and also professional. In turn, a minimally sensitive player would be excited if he really knew the trust that the coach has in him when he puts him in the starting eleven.

It is always an immense act of trust to place your destiny in the hands of others. I myself have to trust that my players, at the end of training, will lead their private lives in a professional way, doing everything necessary and everything I try to teach them to recover as soon as possible and be in the best conditions to train and perform the next day. For the coaches, and specifically for a physical trainer like me, the feeling of having everything under control is just that, a feeling. We don't control anything. We only spend a few hours a day with the player and the rest of the time, during that "hidden training" that is rest and good habits, we do not know anything about what may actually be happening. We are, like when the referee's whistle authorizes the start of a match, at the mercy of the players.

That is why I always do my best, I do everything that is humanly within my power, and then I simply put everything in their hands. From experience and statistics, I already count on the reality that there will always be players who will cheat and even "betray" us, but despite the countless failures, disappointments, and deceptions that I have taken, my attitude is still, ahead of any other, to continue believing in them until they show me that I was wrong. Although, trust is like a paper that once crumpled, no matter how much it stretches, will never be as it was at the beginning when it was immaculately smooth. For this reason, I believe that regaining trust once lost is an act of faith rather than reason, and restoring it becomes, more than anything else, pure commitment.

I also have the total certainty that the success of a team is almost always based on the trust that the group has in their coach. The coach, once his speech is exhausted and his arguments no longer convince, had better pack his bags and leave. It is usually an arduous and expensive task to gain trust which then, at any moment, with a bad word, an inappropriate gesture or a simple wrong act, is over. Stable, free and mature relationships are built on trust. The managers trust the coach they hire, the sports director trusts the players that

Self-Confidence and Trust

they bring, and the coach trusts the assistants they carry with them and thus we must all trust everyone to try to get the projects, in which there are so many resources.

Something as complex as a football club, as a whole, requires high levels of trust in the others as a group. The chances of success of a team are multiplied exponentially when they have a clear, firm, and well-defined joint objective. A real group trust is generated as a product of the individual sum of trust in others, which can be perceived with total clarity when each of its members has security and hope in the capabilities of their colleagues.

For the success of a team, it is necessary to build a solid foundation of trust in the group, where leaders are the example and the first committed. They are the connecting link and guides that form the structure, creating an atmosphere of relationship between the players and helping the youngest or those in need to improve their self-esteem and confidence when they are not sufficiently developed to offer their full potential.

Working as a team is complicated, but there is something that makes it even more difficult in the competitive field of football, and that is the fact of creating a group with bases of mutual trust between individuals, who, in each training session, we are asking to compete with each other. We ask players to trust their teammates, but we demand that they train hard to take the other's job. Therefore, it is also our mission to direct that internal fight well within an ethical and moral framework that guarantees healthy competitiveness, because, at the end of the day, each player fights for his place in the starting eleven and battles against a teammate who will do everything possible to beat him. Although this is paradoxical, the footballer must understand that this situation should make him improve. However, you need the trust that the other always acts in good faith, with integrity and nobility, and is not waiting for your misfortune (such as injury) to achieve their ends. That is why the lack of trust is incompatible with the establishment of constructive and lasting human bonds, generating environments of suspicion and resentment, leading to convoluted situations that endanger the unity of the group.

In a truly cohesive team, you can feel an intense and clearly focused energy, developing its own collective conscience, a strong sense of responsibility, its own codes of behaviour, high levels of openness and its conflict resolution systems making possible the overcoming of the moments of difficulty that always come. Teams with a clear focus have clear and well-defined purposes, maintain, and update the reasons and motives for which they strive, align themselves around a shared and unified vision of their common goals, where each of their members feels equally responsible and important, joining each other by affinities that create synergies that enhance their capabilities through the establishment of solid interpersonal relationships.

Self-confidence always starts with yourself. When I wake up every morning, one of the most important parts of my daily "scan" is trying to pinpoint the exact state of my self-confidence. To be honest, in my case, it's something that seems to have a life of its own; it comes and goes, appearing and disappearing whenever it pleases. Although my relationship with it is generally good and I can count on a reasonable trust normally, I will not deny it – sometimes it abandons me without saying anything, leaving me unprotected, helpless and as if saying "handle it alone". That is something that angers me deep down because I never quite understand why, from one moment to another, it is capable of vanishing. That is why I am very aware of its cycles, I know that it goes seasonally, and I also know that although its acquisition is slow and expensive, it can suddenly leave me without saying a word. We must have a good relationship with our confidence, pay attention to it, work on it, because if we cannot control it in its negative spiral, there are moments in our life when we can go too quickly from confidence to lack of confidence, later to stress and finally, if we do not remedy the situation, to anxiety. And there, we are already talking about important problems.

Everything I have achieved in my life has always started in my imagination, constantly fighting against the indefatigable voices telling me to quit, but as difficult or impossible as it may seem, I have never taken that first step without feeling confident in myself and in my possibilities, that which makes you imagine and leads you to visualize certain situations that are finally undertaken only with the permission of our fears. But fear, dear friend, is another story.

CHAPTER 20

Retirement

Retirement involves many things and can come for many reasons. In this chapter, we are not talking about normal retirement due to age, but that moment in life where you decide to move away from what once was your place, and get out of "the trenches". For most people, when we feel fulfilled in our work, we have been very busy, fighting day by day for the goals and what we believed in, these are beautiful moments to live because you perform as a professional. Yet the day comes when none of that makes sense anymore. You love it and you have given all your passion to it, but the day comes when, for whatever reason, that effort stops making sense. It is a sensation, an inner feeling and that is also usually caused by a context; by experiences.

Retirement as victory or as defeat?

Both cases can occur, after the acceptance of the professional defeat that crosses that limit to the personal and stops being worth it or being important in your life. On the other hand, the feeling of victory or feeling complete in your life with what you have already achieved can cause you to lose the energy to continue completing more "chapters". Apathy and fatigue come, and you need something new to stimulate you.

Both can be motives.

Focusing on the first, we must emphasize that depending on the personality you have, things will affect you in different ways. Especially for passionate, hard-working people, frustration can easily appear because their expectations of themselves and others are so high. When your expectations are very high, you have a greater risk of failing, but, at the same time, if you demand from others the same as you demand from yourself, frustration will come many times, because it is difficult for many people to be able to offer that level of work and effort.

When you get to a point where you try and fight for what you want every day and you don't get your goals, the day may come when you want to avoid suffering and it may be time to quit. The same thing happens to a footballer who, no matter how much he/she does, does not play or does not achieve his/her goals. It is in those moments where people with a strong and resistant character endure because sometimes victory is close, but you don't see it, there is no one who is going to tell you when an opportunity comes or not, so you cannot give up and must believe that it is coming. However, there are also other times when the limits are crossed and the decision to turn the page is made.

It is difficult when we have achieved the objectives and the motivation ends. When we lose motivation, there is only one way to regain it, and that is to create new goals. It takes time, but it can be achieved with the help of your trusted people because there is always something to fight for, even if it is just for your personal happiness.

What? Where are we going?

Life is directed by goals, but it is the path that we really live with intensity, and we must appreciate it more. Once we reach the end, we can feel that everything is done, that we have nothing left to continue fighting for. It is at that moment where the value of maintaining the effort and of gradually finding other things that motivate us must be demonstrated, in that situation or in another. Life can change and not necessarily for the better, but always for the better for yourself, whatever you need and feel. In football, after the goals, it remains to help others to achieve them, to enjoy time for yourself. There are

The Things We Know and Do Not Say

many more things to living, and if you do not know which ones, just ask the right questions and you will get the right answers.

How do I feel about my past and present?
The things that I have done, have they improved my life?
What do I want for my future?
What do I want to improve or change?
What do I want to do?
Where do I want to go?
How can I get it?
Etc.

We must ask these questions of ourselves, but the answers can come from us alone or with the help of our people of maximum trust and support.

Retirement implies a liberation, and many people would say it is a step back, but it is a step forward because it supposes loving something dear; it means leaving the past aside and going back to what we want, desire and, above all, need in our mind and heart. In football, retirement is not usually desired, although there are times when, as we talked about before, we may have achieved everything and are prepared for another life or simply want to change our current life due to a series of bad experiences where the context around the business is usually the problem.

Withdrawal is usually used to define the moment when work stops. Yet working is not the only thing in life; one can retire from more things. It can be done gradually or at once. Quit if that's what you need but we never recommend this, because, in busy moments, you never think coldly about the steps to take forward. The causes can be friends, family, hobbies, places, people in general, goals, etc. But you don't have to be arrogant and should know how to measure the reasons for your decisions, so look in the mirror and bare your soul. Retiring requires inner peace, courage, knowing oneself, respecting oneself, being above what others think and above all, having confidence. The goal is not achieved in a day or two; it takes time and courage to look at what is inside you.

Either way, life is short and retirement, or "change" in your work or personal life, should always be based on a plan, with objectives, goals and with the foundations of a structured and logical life. Nothing good comes from things done too quickly; everything has its stages.

We all know many people who only had work goals and who have a lot of money but have no life and have not done anything they really wanted to do. If we have health, we will live ninety years, more or less, so we must never let our fears or the thoughts of ignorant people control our lives; fear is meaningless. Yet, sometimes we are definitely afraid; afraid of what people could say. Society can make us into something that we do not want to be.

The message is that we will always be directed by that "social message" but we can choose how they have control over us. Please sit down and think about this; analyse your life, what you really want, and then try to get closer to it, because when we die, we do not take anything material from this world, only our experiences.

Retirement and peace.

I think that the most important thing that gives us peace is when we realise that we have experienced what we desire, we did what we wanted and we find ourselves just wanting to go "back home"; we care about family, friends, a match on TV, we begin to appreciate certain things that in the past, were not important for us. This is when we begin to realise what it means to have a real life, and what it means to care about us and what we have. We feel the peace, that place where there is no jealousy, no pain, and no regrets, just another history in this world.

We are talking about appreciating the world, our world, in a real way, through acceptance, adaptation, and calm. A peace that only mature, experienced people understand and who have forgiven others and themselves for the good and bad they have had in their life.

Extra comment/thought/feeling:
Just as we cannot love without loving ourselves, we cannot have peace with others if we do not have peace within ourselves.

CHAPTER 21

Countryside Vs City Life

This chapter has a metaphorical meaning as life in the countryside represents the quiet life, the life in peace where we appreciate things in a more global and, above all, human way. This contrasts with life in the city, where we have created a world where buying and selling and consuming is the basis of life, a life that forgets the human essence and focuses on stimulating our senses in different ways. It is true that with the arrival of the cities, our life changed. The city brings us everything we need, but sometimes too much in terms of stimulation, and we lack that tranquillity that the countryside provides. It is a need for human beings, as we are animals, and sometimes, we have forgotten that.

The human being has created the city, but we come from the countryside, and we cannot forget this fact. We are losing the habits that make us healthy; human, basic things like taking time to think, appreciating a sunrise, helping others, taking care of your health, not being in a rush all the time, etc.

Life is shorter than we think, and it could end at any time. Young people are not taught to appreciate what they have and the context in which they live with respect to others. It is the same in football; time passes, and we believe that we will always be, but the reality is that you will never be the same again. It is our choice to change for the better or for the worse and to help or to hurt the people around us. Not many people have opportunities so when you have them, you should take advantage of them without fear, the fear created by others that we make our own. In that way, you can live life to the full.

Focusing on ourselves: We must talk about what we are and what we are not. We are humans and animals; we are not robots. We need to take care of our bodies and minds, or we will be weaker. The city offers a series of places to meet your needs, needs that, in turn, have been created by brands and companies, as we do not need all the things that they say that we need for living. The countryside will give us the mental and physical tranquillity that is necessary, and that many of us have been denied in a world dominated by the need to buy, have, and consume.

Do we really live the life we want?

An easy question to answer - we always think so, although we do not know if this is caused by external factors or our own. We need to generate critical thinking about ourselves and simply open our minds to know ourselves better and what we need. Learn to look inside yourself and know if you are really doing and feeling what you want to do and feel. We belong to nature but through evolution, we have moved away from it, forgetting what really relaxes us, and what we really are.

The main theme of this chapter is how society influences us. The city presents us with a series of stimuli, making us believe that we need to have and buy many things. The majority of people, through TV and marketing from a young age, really believe that they need to buy that coat or that bicycle, or do something. The countryside, in turn, shows us the simple life, the real life, calm and without stimuli other than the purely human ones. This does not mean that people who live in the city do not have criticism, since we talk about having that critical attitude, whatever the context is, to grow as human beings and not forget what we are, what we need and what we really want. In football, being humble, calm, and focused on our things, is the key to success. We are not talking about the success of what others think about us, but success for you as a person, for what you think of yourself.

We must understand what we need. Sometimes, we need a break, and we don't see it clearly. We never stop to think for a few minutes without noise, to listen to what is happening around us, to listen to the birds or listen to what we think. We live such an organized and busy life that we do not take time for our minds and bodies to rest. As footballers, surrounded by so much pressure on and off the training pitch, we must take care of ourselves, appreciate where we are, and value and feel the day because it could be our last. Take moments to think; sometimes, sitting in the stands to think for a few minutes can give you ideas. It releases you from tension and you merge with the thoughts that you have locked up, but these thoughts don't usually come out with the pressure, the tension, the crowd, the busy life that we have in the city. This is what the city and the countryside represent, that fight between what is manufactured and what is natural, between what is healthy and what is harmful if you cross the border.

The truth is that even if we do not live like two thousand years ago, the countryside and the sea still seem like the best places for vacation, because we can relax and rest, and this is no coincidence. However, I am not writing this because you must go to live in the countryside. I am simply saying that we must not forget what we need, what we feel, and where we come from. This is healthy for us; let's not forget that we are not robots. Respect the people and help them because what you give today, will come back to you tomorrow, and do not forget that in a hundred years, we will all be under the ground; nothing and nobody lasts forever.

The human being is the only animal that focuses his/her entire life on improvement, that's why we control the world, evolution, etc. Yet sometimes it makes you wonder if we should have a balance because we are not sure how we will end if we keep doing this. We are not taking care of the world we live in; we care more about our iPhones than friends, and we also call Facebook contacts "friends" when they are not friends. I am not sure if this is evolution, or if we are going down the wrong path. It is tough to tell this, but it's true; we are more associated with the countryside than we are with IT technologies, but the new generations will not know this fact; they will be born into an era where the new technologies control us, not vice versa.

Look back, learn where we come from, know what the world had in the past, has now, and will have in the future, and live a healthy life, trying to have the peace of mind to decide what you need. Criticize what we have, educate others in good routines and ultimately, help to build a better world and better football.

Extra comment/thought/feeling:
Think how you want your life to be and go for it; just do it. Live YOUR LIFE, not other people's life.

CHAPTER 22

The Science of Positivity

Positivity is a characteristic of many people's personalities, even a talent, and it must be a quality improved and perfected over the years because we must have strategies to be more positive, motivated and, as a consequence, happier. We must understand the environment, but also understand ourselves because happiness begins with oneself. Being positive is an attitude towards life, and it is an attitude towards what we can or can't do, the excuses we make and the way we deal with the problems that we have.

The world is a difficult place but, for those who read this book, or most of you who will have access to this book, you were born in a country with opportunities and at least a little organized. If you are born in a country of this type, or "first world" as it is usually called, you must understand that you are luckier than many people in the world. You were born in a country that will allow you, if you try hard, to have a good life depending on your effort and situation.

If you are born in a country like the UK, it doesn't matter where you come from. If you make an effort, you will always have the opportunity to study and be something in life. It is undeniable that apart from your effort, your situation and contacts will have an influence, but you can have control of your own destiny. This is a reason to be positive, but we must first value it; we must put ourselves in the shoes of those with more problems and fewer opportunities than us.

Now, look at yourself. We can have many problems in life, and it is normal that sometimes we feel bad, but if we are lucky enough to have people around us who love us, like our family, friends, even teachers at school or coaches, we will have immense luck and we must value it. We always have to think that we are lucky to have what we have, and that's why there are always people who are worse off, who have no one, who, even if they want to, cannot and will not grow, just because they were born in a different environment.

Should we feel lucky or not then? Should we be positive about what we have in the first world?

I think the answer is yes, and we would be disrespecting many people if we did not consider it that way.

We also have to think that life could end at any moment, so feeling sorry for ourselves and making excuses for not trying to grow and live the life we desire means that we are afraid of achieving what we could achieve. We have to be brave and go for what we want to achieve because nothing can stop us except our own fears. There will be people who will send you negative messages; listen to close people, but not negative people who will try to convince you that you cannot achieve your goals, just because they cannot achieve their ones. There are many people who are envious and who want to pass their fears on to you. If you want something, going for it and getting it is the only option, because we have limits, but you shouldn't be the one who sets them; let life do that.

Being positive is an attitude towards life, a way of being and feeling your place in the world. Trust yourself, know what you have, value it and go for it without fear, taking steps towards the goal. Always be aware that there will be risks, situations that we will not like and people that we will intimidate because of our mental "strength", but that is secondary. You control your destiny and feeling alive is a personal responsibility that we have to ourselves every day of our life.

The Science of Positivity

In football, we must feel privileged to be professionals. We have a good salary, free time, and the peace of dedicating ourselves to a sport that everyone loves. It must be a joy to get up every morning and that is how we should take it because once we retire, everything will change.

In bad times, we will need to be positive, such as in those moments when we feel bad or tired, alone and aimless. Being positive is good for us but also for others, for the people around us, and we have a responsibility to others as well as to ourselves. Remember in those moments the lifestyle you have, as well as the options, then look at yourself and smile, because if you realize how lucky you are, you will be happy and you will transmit that to others.

Surrounding yourself with positive people is also a reason for joy and a guarantee of success because human beings are affected by what we see in others. If the message is sent out in the right way, we can bring positivity to many people through every step we take and every feeling we express.

It is difficult to be positive every day because we don't have the same feelings, and our feelings guide how we will act in the present, how we talk, eat, listen and behave with others, etc. We should care about things, but we must also relativize life sometimes. We have to focus on trying to be the best we can be, but also not lose time thinking about silly things.

Being positive means showing people what we feel, reacting to things with a smile and treating ourselves as we need to be treated - nicely. You have to love yourself to be able to love others, you have to know how to be happy in order to make others happy; and in every step that we take, we learn how to do this; it's just part of life.

Life is what we have created, and humans have created the routine that we have, and so, it is simply something that has been invented. It is not real, so we can change our life whenever we want; we just need to do it the right way and with a plan. The first thing is to be and feel happy with yourself and with what you have around you, because if not, there is no point in continuing to live that life, and perhaps it would be worth it to make some changes. If I want to change, I just need to have a plan and fulfil it. I must adapt to my environment, of course, but I always have options to improve my life if it is really what I want; what I desire.

Life is not what we can see or what people tell us it is; life is what we do and create around it. Clearly, we need to love ourselves and love what we do on a regular basis. If not, let's take time to think about what's going wrong because it's not worth being stuck in a place, job or relationship if you are not getting anything from it. Sometimes you keep working because of the money, and that's worthwhile because you have a reason to do what you do; what I mean is that there are many people who are stuck in a place or a thing and they don't have any reason for it, so if it doesn't make any sense to you, you should change it straight away. It is not that tough; it just takes time to figure out what you want and how to get it; surround yourself with the right people and go for it. In football, happiness is in the little things, so appreciate them, and keep an eye on the future and the next step.

Being happy is difficult and easy at the same time; we just need to be sure of our desires and go after them. Being positive and appreciating the time God has given us is a gift.

Extra comment/thought/feeling:
Cristian Ramírez Raggio
Engineer and football coach in Milwaukee (USA).

On many occasions, we hear fans, parents, coaches, managers and other people speak about how to motivate a team or person, and positivity is a very important psychological facet for all "motivation".

By motivation, I understand being "positive"; that is, "any behaviour that pursues the achievement of a goal". There are many occasions when we can observe whether a player, depending on the intensity with which he/she wants to achieve these goals, has a greater or lesser motivation. Therefore, we can affirm that a motivated and positive athlete will have well-established goals, will have better individual performance, and will, therefore, benefit the team.

The tone of our message is the key. Used in an appropriate way, the players or people accept certain words, which otherwise would surely be offensive to them. It requires knowing the correct words to be motivated and to feel positively stimulated, and from then, the difficult thing is that they believe in you. As adults, gaining the confidence of young people is tough, but it is essential to listen and be heard in life and make good and bad decisions through which we can learn and remember in our lives.

My philosophy is clear and direct.

Winning is not the only important thing; striving to achieve any goal is also important. Success is doing everything possible to achieve our goals. With effort, we must also instil in children or people the importance of working and improving according to the possibilities of each person, so that in the end, we are always winners.

Promoting this philosophy is complicated by the competitive environment in which we live and by the inevitable comparison with others. Still, the practice of this philosophy will lead people to enjoy any sport, whether or not they are winning. This is what really matters at this stage of learning.

On the other hand, failure is not synonymous with defeat, nor is success a victory. Success is in the daily improvement of our players and in having that desire to achieve and advance in each training based on their initial abilities. Therefore, it is very important to take into account more than the result in these categories. We should also appreciate the effort and skills of all people involved, but the point is we must believe in that challenge from the beginning to the end. In my career, I know that I will continue to learn, but the most important thing for me is to know that I am helping many children to believe in themselves as people and that they feel supported from the beginning to the end.

Be positive, happy and smile.

CHAPTER 23

Values

Values are the foundation of a way of being, living and feeling. They are what makes us ourselves, in a good way and also in a bad way, because nobody is perfect. Values come from home and school, where education is the key. Values shape our character and make us good or bad people. You can also improve as a person, so you can develop these values throughout life.

Values are built from home and the context that surrounds us also plays a key role. Nobody is born knowing anything, acting in one way or another, thus we will learn from what we see and are told. Education is key and teachers, coaches, even a team captain from the school or your football club, all of them have the future of these young people in their hands, because they are the reference point, because they transmit values and this makes education one of the fundamental pillars of a country.

Values have been defined for hundreds of years as the way in which human beings should behave, both among themselves and especially with others. Everything rests on education at home and at school, and so we speak of "education" as the key to the development of a country, of everything. Where education is not considered important, or when teachers are looked on as irrelevant, that is a country without a good future, because it's their citizens and their actions that determine whether it is a good country or not. At home, it is the parents and relatives who have the duty to teach, to educate, but it is also the environment that the child has that is going to help or harm; therefore, we speak of a united whole.

Sport teaches values; this is one of the most important qualities that make sport very important for the education of our young people. It allows them to be in a healthy environment where they learn from a game. That's right - in its origins, sport, including football, must be pure and healthy, where respect and values are the most important and without a doubt it is and will be in the future, a great help, especially in deprived areas.

Aside from sport and values, it is also necessary to promote the love of knowledge, because knowledge and learning will save us and will help us to have a good life.

Nowadays, it has become quite common for young people to ridicule someone who studies a lot.

It seems that you must choose between being studious or being popular at school. So why do we need to be studious or not? Why can't we just try our best? We must know that balance is the key and trying to give your best version in all situations is what will make you great.

Knowledge will save you from being ignorant, which is the most precious asset that human beings have. That is also what differentiates us from animals because the entire animal world can use the physical, but only the human being can analyse and think. Even being a rich player, you should have knowledge because you want to protect what you have gained, and there will be many people trying to rob you. Knowledge is the key to your success in life. This education, this knowledge is the foundation of your values as a person and as a professional.

As we said before, sport is used to help young people with good habits and values, but professional sport is different because it is a business. The move from amateur to professional is a change in the level of the game, but even more in the mentality.

Values

In football, you learn many values, especially the sense of the "team", the sense of belonging to your teammates and being dedicated to your profession. Also, being generous for the common good in any group that fights for a common goal is beneficial and helps the entire team. However, in a dressing room, not everything is good; there is envy and selfishness because each one has individual goals apart from the collective ones. The contracts are individual, and each one has its specific clauses, such as bonuses for goals or number of games played, and contractual relationships that affect not only them as individuals, but their families, etc. Tense situations occur that are normal, but not good from a morale and team point of view. Remember that what you give out will return the same way; if you generate values and positivity, that's what you will receive back most of the time, and vice versa.

Parents and educators have a great responsibility, but so do you as a player, because even if we are young, we have younger people in the academy that are looking up to us, and we are like idols to them. We need to transmit these values from generation to generation, teaching from the truth and not making it too easy for young people. Sometimes putting obstacles in their path will make them stronger, so that in the future, when they have obstacles of their own, they can face them and be successful.

> "The one who truly loves you, will make you cry."
> *(True love or affection consists of correcting the mistakes of a loved one, even if it hurts to do so)*

In professional football, they say that you don't see many values, but it's not true. It is true that there are bad things and bad people, but you also meet great people from whom you learn a lot and experience great moments. Life is full of good and bad experiences, and it is our responsibility to always get the best out of every situation.

Sometimes you must take time and think about what happened in the day, to reflect, as this reflection in a time of peace is very important. Now we are all going very fast and we don't rest. We don't take time for ourselves as everything goes very quickly. Values are learned from a young age, but also when we are older and there is always time to be a better person and improve.

As a football player, you have the responsibility to help young people, because someone helped you in the past, and if they did not, you have to help more, because we cannot blame our bad experiences on other people who do not deserve it. Synergy between people is what makes us great; it is what makes us improve and grow.

Football has its codes, and you can learn a lot from them. It is a great place to acquire the knowledge of facing things together as a team, or as a family. A united team, that feeling of family, is a feeling that when you live it, is the best thing in the world, and it is what you will never forget once you retire. So, please, don't waste your talent or your time - time flies; today you are seventeen and tomorrow you will be thirty.

Extra comment/thought/feeling:
Miguel Ángel Sáez Soriano
Professional Physical Coach. 20 years at Club Atlético de Madrid. Professional Sport Management officer by Madrid County GOV.

The advantage of being yourself.

I have always wanted to learn. I have always been curious to understand the meaning of things, the reason why, and know how it works.

When I trained, the goal was to compete, to grow sportingly, to be better than my rivals and to surpass myself, therefore, each training was a challenge, each competition a goal. When it was time to change roles and become a coach, the lack of experience and youth made me transfer what I had lived and experienced as a competitor, to the programming of my training sessions.

I put my energy into intensity, motivation and achievements, from the conviction that it was the best for the athlete, which was what they asked from me because at the time it was what I wanted, it was what I now see as unidirectional training - I know what I do and I do it well.

Fortunately, on my way, there were professionals who taught me how to learn, not how to train or what to do. They taught me to return to that curiosity, to that phase of understanding things. That is when I began to be part of the training and not the protagonist.

But there was one thing that caught my attention above the rest, something that seemed not to be part of the sport, that did not stand out as a quality to train better. Those professionals, who were in first division teams, the national team, the league, and cup champions, with enviable experience in elite sport, all of them were giving me the opportunity to learn as they shared their experience with me. Why?

They were the same people as when they started, with the same humility as when, like me, they started in the sports world, and they transmitted it that way.

From the beginning, I have wanted to be the same, becoming passionate about everything that surrounds me, knowing that it is important to learn training by training, that everyone can teach you and that everyone can learn. For me, it has been a goal not to lose curiosity, to know that from the pre-youngest stage to the elite, we are dealing with people, and that one of the most important parts is their personal and sports training, with the needs of each stage. I thank my colleagues for all the years shared, since, from each of them, I have been able to learn something. Having the opportunity to be with other professionals and be able to share with them all their experiences, has been one of the best gifts I have had in my sports career.

Sometimes we do not show ourselves as we really are, out of fear, insecurity, or lack of confidence. We constantly want to prove something, and, on many occasions, regardless of the path or what is on it. My conception of training starts from self-confidence, being me for real, and not a facade to prove something, something that is not true and that will be difficult to maintain over time. The advantage of being yourself is that we can be authentic.

I do not want to confuse this with a lack of ambition; I have it, and I believe it is fundamental both for the progression of each one and of those around us. Within a healthy environment, ambition will help all team members to progress. I also like to win and I work for it, but without stopping training to learn, to face all possibilities, including mistakes and defeat as part of that training process.

But I have understood this ambition from the perspective of being part of a team, of a Club, understanding that I am part of a collective and that we all work for a common goal and in a direction, each one with a role, where everyone strives to grow personally and in a sporting way. This is an ambition that leads you to give your best in each training session, in each game, whether you are in a junior, youth or any category team.

It is essential to have values, to be faithful to them, and to be aware of what we do and what we transmit. I enjoy every training session; I find the motivation in choosing to be like that and I have turned my motivation into my values.

CHAPTER 24

Expectations

Great feats are forged in thought, courage, and expectations; it is what makes us believe in our dreams, fighting to achieve them. To have expectations is very important and necessary because we must protect our dreams, and dreams are protected by courage and by believing in ourselves and doing everything in our power to achieve our goals. Expectations offer us the level we want to reach and the level of success we want to achieve, and as long as they do not go over the limit and are on the right track, they are a key part of the plan. Daily work is also the best way to set and control actual and potential expectations.

However, expectations sometimes ruin our motivation and cause our performance or concentration to drop, so we must have correct expectations for every situation. Experience is the key to interpreting situations and understanding contexts, people, and ourselves as well. Knowledge is the best guide we can have in life. If we don't know something, ask, read up on it or study it. The more we know, the better we understand the world and we can better control the contexts.

At the same time, you will also realize that no matter how much we know, we actually know nothing and cannot control anything in this life, so try your best, but also be open-minded enough to enjoy every day, whatever happens. The expectations created by motivation are beneficial in many ways because we need this stimulus that makes us fight for what we want. Football is the same; to know what surrounds a team will be important and will give you calm and category in it. In turn, it can destroy you if your expectations are not adapted to the reality that you live.

You have to have the correct expectations based on realities, but it must be said that it never hurt to have good thoughts about yourself, to feel better than what you really are; self-confidence is so important and makes the impossible sometimes able to be achieved. It also plays a fundamental role in ensuring that we can get the expectations that we have in mind. Yet, at the same time, we must know what we are doing wrong and be realistic so that we can improve.

Expectations are born from our own thinking about something we want or that we are going to try to achieve. They are expectations that are not real, but they have some reality because they are based on past experiences, on people's comments, or on what you have been able to see or watch on TV. Patience is another key because nothing is achieved quickly and easily; we have to believe in the plan and work day by day, having better or worse days, but staying motivated and focused on the plan. Patience gives you the peace of mind to know that everything will come, step by step.

Knowledge, patience and daily work, together with the knowledge of the context and self-confidence, will all turn us into very powerful people of character, incapable of being defeated, even in the worst situations. The fight is non-negotiable because we can win or lose but the effort and sacrifice are non-negotiable; this is the basis of all good character, which supports a goal, a plan and realistic expectations.

There are several types of expectations, in what we want to achieve in our life and also expectations based on people.

We have already spoken about the first, which requires a good mix of self-confidence, patience, courage, knowledge and daily work. But the expectations that we have about people are more difficult and complex because people hurt us more than not achieving personal goals. Life is based on synergies; no one can go through life alone. We are all forced to trust others, to interact with others, to support each other, and from here, good and very bad things come out.

The expectations we can have about our context and about people are very difficult, almost impossible to control. Life teaches you not to expect anything from anyone, it's that simple because when you expect something from someone, that's when they can hurt you. We have to be brave and open up to certain people but opening your heart and mind to everyone will hurt you because even though it is sad, we cannot trust everyone. Even so, life will teach you based on experiences; we all have those and nobody escapes from them. Life is not easy and the fact is that it's impossible to trust everybody. People will hurt you in many ways and they will not care about it, just because we focus firstly on ourselves and then the rest.

The expectations we have of people can vary – sometimes they are many and at other times very few. This is because there are some wonderful people in the world, but there are also evil people so you have to be very careful. To have the ability to judge, even if it is difficult, and even if we have misjudged someone, never completely close yourself off from people since, although we should be careful, closing ourselves off completely would destroy us as we always need to have faith.

Also, the culture we have come from will affect how we treat others and how we feel about them. There are countries where people are more open-minded and used to be more friendly in the beginning, but later on, they betrayed others easily without any kind of regret. We need to think about which people to let into our world. When you are young, it is normal to let more people in, and then we change when we are getting older because we get that experience and we learn about life.

We need to trust people when they deserve it; we are talking about give and take here. Some people just take and never give, so that is where we should stop it and not let people cheat on us. Where is the limit? That's the key and we have to make a decision about it; balance is the key here – try to be open-minded about everyone to start with and then you can choose who you open up to.

People will disappoint you again and again, because the human being is selfish by nature, and this is due to the 'survival of the fittest' teachings from prehistory. Back then, no one gave anything for anyone, nor did anything for anyone. We were selfish and bad people, but we did not realize that a group is stronger than being alone and that sharing knowledge, experiences and life with others makes us better and improves our lives.

On the other hand, some prefer to envy others, which makes us gradually destroy ourselves and nobody wins anything. It is an absurd way of living, but it is what we have chosen and what brands and films have taught us; to go with the "individual" not the "collective." Brands and advertisements show how to present ourselves as people who are arrogant, without appreciating anything and with signs of dissatisfaction with everything that is around. This does not help to create good people, people who believe in companionship, help others, work for the common good, etc.

This indoctrination of our ideas can be dangerous so we must be aware and wary of allowing ourselves to be taught these principles.

It is tough to pass this information to others, especially young people, to whom we are constantly striving to pass on positivity, but this is the world where we live, so we need to make sure that our youngsters know it sooner rather than later so that they don't make the same mistakes that some of us made in the past, just for thinking that we could change things or change people.

In football, as in life, you will have few friends, even within your own family. Sometimes you can even count them on the fingers of one hand. Trust yourself and your close circle of friends. When it comes to others, my advice is that you do not trust anyone and always be very careful with the expectations you have of people. Regarding our personal expectations, we must always aim for ten out of ten or at least a nine, because if I aim high, even if I don't get it, at least I will be close. Believe in yourself, be organised and go for it, because in life and in football, you can achieve everything you set out to do, but it depends on you.

The final message is to highlight the importance of believing in yourself. Plan big and, most importantly, dream big with high expectations and put the same level of effort into them. We must have our trustworthy people, but don't worry about others. Just stay away from negative people who do not contribute anything to us. If you believe and fight, you can achieve everything you desire.

Extra comment/thought/feeling:
Your energy, as well as your expectations, must come from yourself. There is no one who can generate anything in you if you don't really believe in it.

CHAPTER 25

Top Business Life

Footballers have a very atypical life because if you are lucky, you can start earning a lot of money from a very young age. How to manage it is the key and, for that reason, we need to have knowledge, surround ourselves well and know about the business. Understanding the context and how to save, maintain and make your money grow is the secret to avoiding bad investments or people stealing what you have earned. Knowledge is key, but business requires ninety percent logical thinking and common sense.

Understanding the context is important, and it is something that is repeated in this book, but it is true - knowledge is the only way to be independent and successful in life. In order to manage money and invest it well, you must have the knowledge acquired by years of minimal studies, and above all by common sense. Many footballers do not know what taxes are, what is net and gross, what you have to pay when buying a house, what a notary is, what the stock market is if you invest in mutual funds, etc. It is essential to know all this and to have people by your side to help you to manage it. But the first thing is always your knowledge and common sense because you are the one who should guide those who help you and not the other way around. Because if you do not understand where you are investing, you will never have control over your assets, and they are yours, you have earned them and you have a responsibility towards yourself and your own effort. To have people helping or giving you advice is one thing, however, letting them handle everything is not good; you should be in charge.

The first thing that should be controlled is your income, expenses and living according to your means, without spending more than you earn. Spend to live comfortably but always save an amount, which allows you to be calm if there is a problem. This is common sense; nobody needs to study to know that if you spend more than you earn, you can have a problem. Always saving something is key because you never know what can happen.

What is a comfortable life?

A comfortable life is one that allows you to have "quality" in everything you need, within limits and without being too extravagant. A comfortable house, healthy food, the possibility of doing sports, having an adjacent green area or near parks; all these things make your life comfortable, calm and with the comforts of the 21st century. Purchase according to what you earn, so, if you earn more, you can have more things; if you earn less, you can have fewer – balance is key.

How much do I save, and how and in what do I invest the savings?

It depends on the salary you have and if you live alone or with someone else, but being able to save 50% of your salary would be ideal. Obviously, there will be extra expenses on certain dates, which will occur due to misfortunes or positive events, but being able to save at least half of what you earn will give you a good base where you can invest the rest. We must obtain the correct advice, either from trusted people, or personal or external advisers, whether of funds or investment groups. Nowadays, you can invest in many things, whether they are service businesses, houses for a real-estate portfolio or simply the option of getting an annual return on your money by investing in mutual funds. There are many options, but for everything, the key will be your own knowledge. Even with the best people by our side (which we will rarely have), we must know the context in which we invest and understand where we are putting our money.

We start talking about knowledge and we end with the same; never invest in something that you cannot control. If you do not know something, learn about it and be able to handle it even if you have people who are experts in it. In life, you don't need to have three careers to live it well, you just need to learn, be humble, have an open mind and, above all, have common sense.

Business life can be easy and difficult at the same time. People with money come from different backgrounds, so they are also different. Once you interact with the people who move money in any industry, you realize that in this life and in any industry, money and contacts are the main things in this world, especially if you want to grow or at least maintain your position. Being humble and knowing how to listen is very important so that later, you can analyse and make decisions. As has already been said in this book, keep your thoughts to yourself, and at most, share them only with those you trust wholeheartedly.

Nobody is better or worse for owning more or less money and you have to know that the more you have, the more people will want to steal it from your pockets, so you must keep your eyes open and be smart enough to keep it. Therefore, you will have to know how to invest it and protect it better, being smarter than them. Nobody is born being nothing; we make ourselves like that, and it is possible to live very well with little if you are organized and intelligent. So, do what you desire, but keep your mind in place and create a balance between today and tomorrow that allows you to maintain a stable, pleasant life.

We are talking about being in control of your life and making it come true. Since we were born, we have been merely "students", and even if we don't have parents or friends to teach us, the world is there in front of us and it comes towards us, so, you must be prepared to face it because, at the end of the day, we are alone. You don't need a lot of money to enjoy life; you just need to work, maintain, control and spend it at the right time and on good things. A good manager of his/her money does not become a good manager by wearing suits; you have to "be" and not "appear" in life, that must be your true self, the one who "is". In front of people, "appearing" is important for your public image, but for yourself, it is what you really are that matters.

A professional career is based on working, having contacts and controlling the context. We cannot be successful if we are alone; we always need people to help us and also to provide another vision of the same event or problem. We are not talking about using people to your advantage, but this world is about synergies and that makes a normal person a businessman, being able to adapt to circumstances, benefit from others, etc.

A business person also needs to have personality and courage to be aware of the world in which he/ she is. The world is what it is and it will not change for you or for your thoughts, so accept the things you see, even if you don't like all of them. Sometimes you will see things which will make you feel bad and you will think about changing your way, but it depends on each person what kinds of things they are capable of facing.

You will find many people who do not mind "selling their own mothers" to get a better salary or a better job. If you are not like that, you will be a good person but be careful because the world will not be like you. The world is a difficult place and you will need to handle all types of situations. You have to go step by step and never give up for any reason. My advice is that you have to feel proud of yourself, so we must never lie or destroy anyone to win anything. The work and the contacts that you get for your own value are the only way to success for a true winner. The "how" we get things done is also very important.

We must be able to transmit knowledge to others about what we achieve in life. We have to find and be able to distinguish real people, people without masks, people with honour, like you. Being a good man/woman is helping others, and that makes you a winner, a confident person, a business person, an open person, self-confident, intelligent; being arrogant never makes you anything.

Extra comment/thought/feeling:
Life is a jungle; trust few people, always be prepared and stay calm to allow you to think clearly.

CHAPTER 26

The Betrayed

The hard thing about betrayal is that it is only caused by people with whom we keep a minimum of trust. If we don't share anything with people, then we cannot feel betrayed. That is why it is the worst thing that can happen to us in life. We are social beings but we let just a few people enter our world, and if one of those people betrays us, it is the worst emotional feeling that can happen to us. It is very hard to think that a person you love and that you would give everything for might betray you, but that is life, and we must be prepared and have a good mindset for it.

The most important thing to say is that if you betray someone, you are betraying yourself first. Betraying implies breaking the given trust, and not having the principles, values or strength to maintain what you said one day you would do. Every day, we care less about honour or having principles, but at a professional level, it is very important to have these characteristics, because it is the difference between someone who can be trusted and someone who cannot. When the betrayal comes from a friend, relative or close person, it is even harder but you have to know how to continue; it's a fundamental rule in your professional life.

When a close person betrays you, you do not know what to feel because the relationship and any confidence gained are totally lost. You won't know why and you won't understand how someone you considered close could do that. It is a terrible feeling that no one should ever experience. Because the human being is a social being by nature, he/she needs the interaction with other human beings to be happy. It is not possible to be a hundred percent happy being alone because we were not born to be alone twenty-four hours a day.

Therefore, be aware of how to face events like this, and know how to move on, maintaining your peace and self-confidence. Terrible things can happen, but if you can maintain some peace and self-confidence, you won't get depressed and can find a way to move forward.

How do you keep trusting people if they betray you once?

Life changes and we have good and bad experiences that should help us improve as human beings and better understand our environment. We should understand and adapt, but not be afraid or lose courage, because not trusting anyone is cowardly. Brave people learn and adapt, letting others come into their lives, and from there, the actions of the people are selected and analysed, so, in the end, you know who your friends are because there are always good people in this world, and there always will be. You have to take the risk of opening your heart and although sometimes you lose, many more times you will win and attain the friendship of honest people.

Life is a mix of good and bad experiences, and we cannot let a bad experience with someone ruin us or change our personality. It is a principle of life that no one changes what you are because otherwise, the world will always get worse. The way to win is to ignore the bad people until they are alone; if they do not cross the threshold, do not confront them directly. Ignoring is wise, revenge is weak, so don't be like them.

How do you adapt, get out of the situation and make yourself stronger?

Getting out of a bad experience is easy; the difficult thing is not falling in again, but it is life and anything could happen. We cannot control everything and you need to learn from the bad in order to improve the next time. This is the way life is for us just now, so we need to learn to remain calm in an ever-changing world.

Football is a good place to learn what betrayal is because football is like a big cake that everyone wants their piece of; the only difference is that some will use very bad weapons (lies) to get their piece. In my opinion, winning is important but the "how" matters, so winning is not everything. Getting up in the morning and feeling good about yourself is very worthwhile. You have to love yourself and you must have honour, which many people do not have. Don't be like them and remember this phrase - "the best punch is the one that doesn't happen". Be ready to win without wasting time with bad people. Beat them with the mind rather than physically, because that is the only way we differ from the animal kingdom.

There is another type of betrayal - this is where you see the kind of person you are, and the person you want to be. There are many times when we find ourselves in situations where our principles are compromised; where what we should do and what we want to do are not the same and our honour and values are compromised. If you cross the line, you don't betray anyone, but you do it to yourself, which is even worse sometimes. There are many difficult situations in life but we must try to keep to ourselves what we say, think and above all, feel. We can make mistakes, which is part of life; yes, making mistakes is normal, but not learning from mistakes has no excuse. Sometimes, looking the other way implies being an accomplice to what is happening. We must value all situations and although we have to think of ourselves first, let's not forget about others, because it is in those moments of doubt that we will see what kind of person we are.

A person with honour is forged from conscience and values. Betraying implies betraying yourself and all that you are. It is up to each one to be the best version of himself/herself or not. Having enough courage to achieve your goals without lying or betraying anyone is to be a real person.

Betrayal is intrinsic to the human being, as is the survival instinct, which makes us think only of ourselves and which directly affects being selfish. It happens easily but is difficult to process, especially when it involves friends or those close to us. How to face these things and especially learn from them, is what will make the difference. In football, it will happen continuously, so, as we have already discussed, being careful what you say and knowing who you can trust are essential to our personal and professional success.

Extra comment/thought/feeling:
Ito Toledo
Former Professional Footballer at Tenerife FC and CD San Isidro. 3rd Division Coach and professional football agent. Director of R14 football Agency. Expert in Canary Islands football.

In football, words like betrayal, teamwork and leadership are in common use. It is not easy and everyone cannot be a leader, but for me, the word is not "leader" or "captain" - the word is family, friend or someone who gives his life for his team, someone who will always stand up as a wall to protect his team and that can only be gained by deeds. Over time, when everyone sees that you give respect and that your team respect you, you will get the group to listen to you and the twenty-five or thirty players in the locker room will go with you to the end without looking back. In the end, if you are a good person and create a family within the team, you will create something that is essential in achieving the goals that are set, because for me, both in sports and in life itself, in any job, the key part is the union – being a family - and knowing that your teammate is going to give his life for you, and on a football pitch, that means a lot, creating a good atmosphere between teammates.

You have to act with heart; be honest and treat everyone equally without neglecting anyone, and, above all, be humble and know how to treat each member of the locker room, because each person is different. Each person needs different things, so we must be attentive to understand these differences in a team. It is a bit of psychology and because of it, you need to have a life experience with situations that pushed you to the limit and made you mature. Sometimes, we focus on the superficial part of things, when the greatest tool in all facets of life is humanity and the closeness you have with people and knowing how to take them to heart, with a hug, a look or a simple gesture.

Football is hypocrisy, falsehood, mistrust, pride, a world of little humility, toward which you feel hatred and, at the same time, love it. There is no explanation; you just have that feeling - you love it and hate it at the same time.

I was prepared from a young age for a specific thing; therefore, I was only prepared to be a footballer and I say it with hand on heart, I do not know how to do anything else in my life other than being a footballer. Due to the circumstances of life, I have had to reset myself and learn to survive and pull ahead in another way. I also owe that strength to football, because my strength of mind came from what I learnt from football. Sometimes, however, it seems that I am not strong and that I have no motivation, but it is like a game; when I am lost, I could starve myself for a day because of anger, but then I would restart my head and continue. On a Monday, I was already thinking about the next game; this has made me stronger, and today, I always have the strength to fight the next day. Yet they never prepared me for tomorrow. I have ex-colleagues who have tried to commit suicide, while others took drugs. Many people betrayed me when I lied to help them. You live in a world of lies - there are good people, but there are more bad ones and interested people who are only there to take advantage of you. The world of football is a messy world and you need to know this if you want to participate in it.

Football has no memory. One day you have everyone behind you, telling you that they love you and the next day you are alone. Step by step, I became stronger within myself and worked on whatever I could but after I quit football, I didn't want to work in the game anymore. I forgot all those negative friendships. Today, I only have four friends but they are good people and real friends. I have no contact with the rest; they have tried to get me into many groups of ex-footballers and I have left them all. I don't want any contact with certain people.

In the end, life gave me the most important lesson that it could, that I will never stumble again, and I also learned many things about myself and what I needed. After a few years, I tried to go back to football and I had problems because the past haunts you, and certain people don't change but I had and I no longer admitted certain things, so you end up being the bad guy when you're the only good boy.

Now, I try to help young people. I tell them about my experience and even their parents cry. The most important thing is to tell young people never to give up and not to waste their talent. There are people who will want to hurt you and who feel good about hurting others. You have to understand it and fight for yourself and for the people who really love you. People have to earn your trust.

My experience started very early; they said that I was one of the promising ones in Tenerife football. At the age of thirteen, I debuted in the Under-19 honour division. Being under fifteen, they took me in the youth team of the Canary Islands to the Spanish championship. I went to all the Spanish championships from Under-15 to Under-19. There were three or four footballers in Tenerife who did that. I was going to sign for Real Madrid but my father did not want to pay for the plane tickets, so they didn't close the deal; life is sometimes hard if you don't get any support.

My life and football taught me many things. In football, betrayal is common- in order to be able to grow in this business, eighty percent of the people betray somebody - it is just a world of egos. Footballers will always ask you, "Where do you come from?" meaning that if you have not played pro, you are nothing. It is a very closed world in which everything passes through the hands of certain people, or you enter into that hypocrisy of congratulating yourself along with people you don't like. Everyone criticizes each other. It all depends if they let you enter their world or not. If you enter, you are protected; if not, it's impossible to survive. Everything moves in cycles.

It is a lonely world and there are no friends. You have to surround yourself with your people and there are times when you cannot trust anyone because to grow in the business, people would even sell their own families. You have to find people like you, good and faithful people, who cannot be bought for anything and who never abandon you. Unfortunately, good people do not usually succeed and it is bad people who do.

The people who know how to betray are the ones who unfortunately succeed because they manage people according to their own interests. When good people realize how everything works, they leave the business because it is not their way of doing things, so bad people always find it easier to stay in the business. There are also people who will discredit you for fear that you know more than they do; it bothers them that you are above them. But the worst thing is that they don't have the desire to learn in order to improve and compete against you; they just want to be there doing nothing and without any training or skill.

In the end, everyone wants to stay on the crest and everyone will look for the smallest detail to discredit you so that they can continue in their position. In football, there are few values; very few have them and those who do have them are called "crazy". Well, I tell you one thing; I would prefer to die a madman than be like these people. For me, this is called leadership, and leadership is earned by actions, not words, and the footballer feels that and perceives it when you talk to him face to face. You either have it or you don't; it is as simple as that.

CHAPTER 27

Decision

Making decisions requires wisdom and character. Wisdom is gained over the years with experience, while character is acquired from a very young age and depends on the context from which you come. The context will mark if you are a soft or hard person from a young age, although you can always improve or change for the worse in the future.

How to improve my wisdom?

It takes time, the desire to learn and above all, admitting your own mistakes. We can only start to change something when we realize that something is wrong. It is often our own ego that prevents us from seeing reality and criticizing ourselves. So, the key would be to be both critical of ourselves and open-minded, then we will get that knowledge and just time will mark our path in life.

Can you improve your character?

Nobody is born with character; it is acquired from a very young age, but we can improve it if we realize what we need to acquire or what we lack. In general, we need a balance of everything - sometimes being aggressive, other times shy, and most of the time being a calm person, controlling the environment and what is happening around us. Character is gained from learning, exactly from listening, seeing and analysing.

Decisions can be made with the mind or the heart. Being guided by the heart is human but not recommended. The mind controls reasoning, the only one that judges without being based on feelings

Decision

or emotions, which is how most of us should guide ourselves. The heart will have to be used but only in situations where your values are compromised by a rational decision, and it is going against yourself and who you really are. However, for the rest of the time, it is the mind that must govern what we are and what we do with clarity and patience.

At the last moment, you need the courage to make the decision and not look back, so just think about the past; if you can improve something you did wrong or learn for the future, then that's fine, but if not, it is not worth it. It is also true that even if we make decisions that we think are the best, many times we will make mistakes and nothing happens, hence learning is the answer to the problem. The character is formed by good decisions, but also by bad ones; nobody is perfect.

If I make a mistake, will my personal confidence drop?

Making mistakes is normal, so, as we always say, learning from mistakes is the key. Your self-confidence may drop, but it depends on you, on your own personality and how hard you are. Above all, you have to consider that if you have made a decision based on a long thought and everything is well thought out, you should be calm about the work done and just keep trusting yourself. However, if the decision was based only on an impulse based on emotional issues without counting on the rational factor, there we must consider what part of the blame we have. When a decision has been made from the mind and has been analysed in detail, we should not blame ourselves for anything, so just learn from it and continue on our way.

In football, decisions will lead you to go through many sensations and emotions, because no one knows everything, so we will make many mistakes. Surrounding yourself with good people is key, but so is understanding the context and trying to know everything. Letting others control your life is the easy but dangerous way in the long run. Trying to learn involves effort, but gives you the peace of mind that you are controlling your things. Follow what reason tells you and don't look back; go on with your life and improve day by day.

Decision-making is not easy because it implies believing in yourself and your context; it implies having no control over something, but assuming it and accepting it with confidence. We have to adapt our minds to the changes of life, because these changes are going to be in front of us when we have to make decisions and we need to face them. The decisions are based on our thoughts, feelings and experiences of the past and it is not easy to do it, but every single year, we get more reasons to believe in what we decide and the path that we choose to take, because we gain more experience.

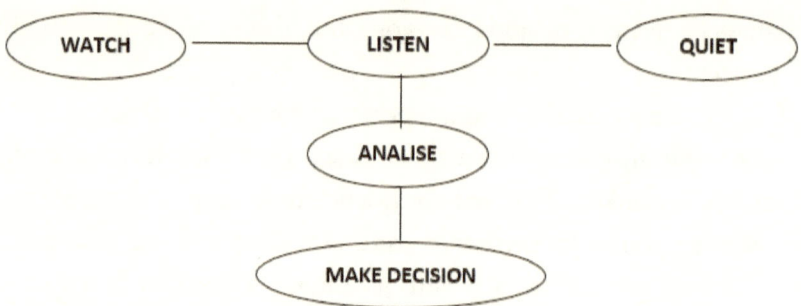

Experience provides the chance to analyse things better, or it should be that way. However, even with all the knowledge about a topic, nothing can ever be assured, because there is nothing sure in life. It is important to understand why we are in this world, what we like and what we want to do. We must forge a strong personality without complexes, then that will make us strong in the face of all the tests and problems of life. Understanding the context, but also ourselves is key because the first mystery of life is understanding who we are.

In football, you will have to make many difficult decisions - club changes, contracts, agents, and decisions related to your life on and off the pitch, which will affect your personal life. Use your mind to analyse every detail, do not trust anyone, listen to the advice of good people, and have the courage to be humble, learn from mistakes and never look back at the past, but forward to the present and future.

Extra comment/thought/feeling:
Pedro Ejzykowicz
Engineer and Economist in Denver (Colorado, USA).

Decision-making.
Definitely something that I'd consider a learning process.
My wife tells me that one should not regret a decision that has been made. I think that it is wise advice, but one that can be hard to apply. If you think the decision you made was not the right one, try to learn from it but move on.
One aspect of decision-making that I think is important has to do with not making any decisions when presented with difficult choices or procrastinating. Keep in mind that not making a decision is a decision too.
It is important to remember that decisions can have consequences, thus, make sure you hold yourself accountable.
I do believe that one should live a life full of experiences, and, in order to do so, one will be faced with multiple decisions over time.
Don't dwell on decisions that are not relevant since the decision-making process can create stress and/or anxiety. On the other hand, there will be important decisions that require one to reflect and consider their potential consequences so don't rush if you think that you need time to evaluate your options. Asking close friends, mentors and family members you trust can be extremely valuable. More often than not, you have time to think about the decision you are faced with. If, for some reason, you do need to make a quick decision, trust

your gut; it will likely be guiding you in the right direction and if you are living a life full of experiences, you will probably be just fine.

Remember not to regret decisions that you have made, but rather, learn from them and embrace the moment you are living with happiness.

Good luck on your next decision!

CHAPTER 28

"Education vs Ignorance"

Education forms the foundations of a country, and it is the topic which helps citizens to be real human beings. It can be used and has been used as a weapon to dominate the crowd because education implies acquiring knowledge and when you deny that to people, they become ignorant and easily led and will follow you like sheep without question.

We are different from animals because we are able to analyse, learn and improve our skills in order to be smart. Education gives us a platform to change the world and it also helped to shape the modern world that we can see today, with all the comforts. Therefore, investing in education means investing in young people who are the future of the nation. Moreover, if a person is educated, he/she will be able to get a degree and a better job, then more money and that will increase the national income of the country. Also, educated people are better citizens in terms of being aware of the duties and responsibilities that they have as citizens and as a part of a nation, so it benefits everybody all round.

The education of young people in a country is also important in order to have citizens who are at ease with critical thinking, real people who don't need a guide to choose their path in life. Unfortunately, we cannot say that we live in that world because we don't. We live in a world where since we were born, we have been trained not to criticise anything, just to buy things or to follow some stereotypes created by companies and the interests of other people. But, having a critical attitude is the basis of education, because to improve as a society and to improve myself as a person, I need to criticize what surrounds me, and criticize myself as well. For all of this, I need knowledge, previously acquired through education, for, in the end, everything is related to everything.

Education is what provides human beings with tools that allow us to discern where our life is going and where we want to go. You will have many people who will tell you what you should or not do, but with knowledge, you will know how to make your own decisions, always based on facts and lessons learned. Without education, ignorance is the owner of your destiny, along with the people around you because if you are ignorant, they will try to manage your decisions.

Education is the pillar on which our beginnings and our lives should be based because nobody gets to know much about anything without it and it is very important to continue learning. Whatever you work on, everything evolves, changes and improves. The important thing is to be in control of your life and your destiny, and that is done only with a good education. Education allows you to have control of your own life, or at least to have more control than we would have if we did not have it. Ignorance is used by bad people to deceive and direct the lives of others. This is the reason why there are many countries that do not promote having a good educational system because they need this ignorance to continue acting as they do. It is our responsibility as individuals, fathers, mothers, etc., to demand it and, if they do not give it to us, to obtain education through our own means, because education can save our lives.

There are two problems in relation to this topic; there are many people who are ignorant and do not know it, and there are others who want to be ignorant because they have suffered so much in their lives that they prefer to live in ignorance. The people who do not

"Education vs Ignorance"

know that they are ignorant are the majority; in fact, the one who speaks the most is always the most ignorant. When a person truly knows a lot about life or about a topic, he/she has already realized that deep down, he/she still has a lot to learn and improve. People who think they know everything are the most ignorant in the world and, in those cases, we know that their education has failed.

As we said before, there are also people who prefer to live in ignorance, because this is the best way not to feel pain. It's much easier to not know what's happening, so they are happy. If these ignorant people can be so happy to live like that, ask yourself the question; is it good to be an ignorant person? After all, being ignorant of the unfair things that surround us provides an easier life. This fact is hard to say but it is true, so why should we keep trying to improve the world? The first thing to say is that these people are ignorant because they chose that way of life. They could have been educated and used critical thinking. In the end, nothing can be done if someone wants to withdraw from the world.

Although educating yourself is good, when you get a certain level of knowledge, the things you see and those that happen around you hurt more. So, where do these words lead us? These words lead us to know just where we are and to be ready for the future because it is not really clear where we are going. It is a sad fact but true that some educated and clever people no longer want to know what is happening around them. This could be for a few reasons; family, work, relationships, etc., problems that make your life miserable and lead you to hide yourself from others. It is understandable and fair to let somebody be happy alone and let that person hide to avoid feeling pain, but we should help these people by pointing out the good in life, not just the bad things happening around them.

Depression is a huge problem these days and it is playing a large role in mental illness, so we should try to educate these people on how to live, how to be tough and have mental strength and how to balance out their way of thinking so that they are not overwhelmed by the things happening around them.

Education is not only knowledge; it also teaches us a way of behaving, manners, a way of treating people and dealing with issues both good and bad. In football, understanding the situations and how to face them is a major factor. It teaches you how to behave in a locker room, being a captain or having one, codes, relationships with the management, agents, media, the environment, etc. Understanding how to be calm, being in your place and controlling your emotions plays a key role in being able to face the things that happen on a day-to-day basis.

Remember that you only own what you keep quiet about, and knowing who is with you and who is not is key. You do not have to use anyone or lie about anything, but you should know how to take people where you want them to go, carefully, tactfully and causing a good impression on others. Football and the experiences you have helps educate yourself and learn about life and relationships. Taking advantage of this knowledge is key to getting there, but especially for staying in business. I find it important to analyse my environment and people, to be open and not cause confrontations, always to know my place and to make the most of opportunities to my own benefit.

When you are in the "football bubble", everything seems great and everyone is interested in you, but sooner or later, that changes and we must know the situation in order to face it before it happens. That is why knowledge and studying, even studying and a career at the same time, will help you to always have a plan, no matter what happens. That is why studying is so important because it gives you the knowledge and education that living in society requires, where each individual has their own problems and they make everything interrelate. It is important to be adaptable but I can only do it if I have the means. It is very important to pass on what you know to the next generations; synergies help to "pass on the knowledge" and preserve what others managed to understand in the past.

Education will make you the owner of your life, and that is something very precious, so try to be always learning, improving day by day, and listening to wise people. If you are playing in a club and you have free time, studying at the same time, these are things that can improve your life especially if you do them at a young age. I guarantee that your life will be yours because knowledge is key and education is everything.

Extra comment/thought/feeling:
The more one knows about something, the more ignorant one realizes one is. It's impossible to know about everything, so thinking you're wise is literally a very stupid thing to do.

CHAPTER 29

Failure

Failure is a term widely used today to define a person who, in the eyes of society, has not become "successful." Next comes the criticism of the person who has failed because right now, if you reach a final and don't win, you're a failure; there is no prize for second place. That is what they tell us, and that is what they teach to children.

The question is, what does it mean to be successful? Who defines what it is to be successful?

There should be no definition of what is successful or not, because for some people, being successful means earning money, for others, the work ambition, while for others, it is simply having a family and living a quiet life. Each person is different, but society tells us what we should aspire to, what is the concept of beauty, goals and even what success means. But we must be the ones who define our own success and future.

Success should be the pursuit of happiness, finding it and actually achieving it in all the aspects that one wishes. Therefore, we could talk about standards, but happiness and the meaning of success will be different for each person. Success should not be the money you earn, but the goals set in all areas, both professional and personal. Without a doubt, a mixture of goals achieved and money that allows you to live well is a good combination. Happiness is a set of factors, experiences and feelings, but every person's conception of happiness is different, based on their successes and environment.

Failure

Failure is often based on a mixture of facts and feelings, the facts being a product of experiences in life, goals achieved or not, concerns and other actions that make up our history in the world. The feelings also matter because not all human beings give the same value to things and therefore, what for me is a failure for another can be a triumph; it depends on expectations and especially on the good or bad experiences that have occurred in the past. Although the events of the past cannot be changed, the feelings I have towards them can be more or less positive.

It's a fact that failure should not be understood as such. If you have tried and done everything you could, it should not be considered as something negative, because life is a sum of experiences. In life, succeeding not only depends on you, you must do your part, but succeeding depends on moments, being in the right place at the right time, meeting people like you and also finding a suitable context. Therefore, calling yourself a "failure" for trying hard and not achieving something is not correct. However, if you do not give everything for your goal and you want to achieve things effortlessly, then you may feel that you have failed at that moment. Not giving everything means not loving or showing a desire to really achieve the goal, and that is a personal failure.

In life, there are many types of people and you have to respect what each one wants. However, giving less than what you can give is sacrificing the gift, that gift that is the effort that we all can give. To "fight" makes you feel alive in what you do and where you are going. If you believe and desire something, if you really put all the effort into it, you will get it; and if you don't get it, nothing happens. Another opportunity will come, but your consciousness will always be very high. Remember that things happen for reasons that we do not know, and also, when one door closes, another always opens.

Since the effort you make is always dependent on you and what you want for yourself, so too, failure always depends on you. A person who feels respect for himself/herself, dignity and personal honour, would never stop fighting to the end for a goal. So, teach and transmit what self-love is and the joys of having goals to fulfil and remember that everything depends on what you are willing to give for your goal.

Failure can destroy a person deep inside and there are many factors that help make it happen, e.g., what you think of yourself, if you give importance to what others think of you, if you have real goals in life, etc. All these reasons and others determine how you feel about your life. We need to find ourselves in this life, otherwise, we will be lost; you need to know who you are and be proud of it and live by your own work and personality, and that way, you can never fail.

Failure is something invented to create a bad feeling inside of us, making us afraid to do things, to try things. The fear of failure puts a barrier around us; a wall that prevents us from having the courage to try to achieve our goals. It is very important to understand that fear is an invention - it is not real - you put it on yourself. Forget your fears and fight, since if you lose, nothing happens. There will be another occasion; this makes you always a winner, whatever happens. In football, it's the same - don't think about others, think about yourself and what you can do. If you have tried your best, whether you succeed or not doesn't matter. You can never be a failure if you have done everything you could.

The reality is that nobody knows everything, so nobody can tell you that you will not achieve something. Analyse your life and your desires and if you want something, keep trying because there is always a way to be successful; you will never be a failure for trying. Many players make excuses and blame other people, which does not mean that they are often wrong. However, excuses don't help anyone and they will never help you. You are the owner of your actions, and it is your actions that will make you feel good about yourself or feel that you have failed. A person who fights and does his/her job every day will be a winner, and that is the only truth that exists.

In football, you have to be smart, and if you really want to be a footballer, try everything to achieve it. However, it is very important to study at the same time, not as plan B, but always as plan A, because studying and knowledge are key. From there, follow this advice; do not be afraid and go for it with all your strength, then, whatever happens, you will have been successful.

Examples of famous people and failure:

Abraham Lincoln
American statesman and lawyer who served as the 16th president of the United States.

Prior to becoming President of the United States, he failed three times in business and failed seven times campaigning in politics.

Albert Einstein
Nobel Prize Physicist who developed the "theory of relativity".

Until he was four years old, he did not talk. His parents considered him "sub-normal." His professors branded him as "mentally slow" and expelled him from school.

Michael Jordan
Former basketball player. Considered the best basketball player of all time. 6 NBA Rings. 14 MVP.

Due to a "lack of skill," he was cut from his high school basketball team.

Bill Gates
American business magnate, software developer, investor, and philanthropist.

Was a Harvard dropout whose first start-up, Traf-O-Data, failed miserably.

Thomas Edison
American inventor and businessman who has been described as America's greatest inventor.

He was told by his teachers that he was "too stupid to learn anything."

Steve Jobs
Chairman, chief executive officer (CEO), and co-founder of Apple inc.

After being fired from the company he founded, he was saddened and depressed at the age of thirty years old.

Oprah Winfrey
American media executive, actress, talk-show host, television producer, and philanthropist.

Her position as a reporter was terminated because she was "unfit" for television.

The Beatles
Famous rock band.

Decca Recording Studios rejected them, stating that "they have no future in show business."

Marilyn Monroe
Actress.

Her producer informed her she wasn't pretty or talented enough to be an actor, therefore, she was dropped by 20th Century Fox after one year.

Walt Disney
American entrepreneur, animator, writer, voice actor and film producer.
A publication fired him for "lack of imagination" and having "no unique ideas."

Henry Ford
American industrialist and business magnate, founder of the Ford Motor Company.
At the age of fifty-three, he was a failure in three businesses until eventually succeeding with Ford Motor Company.

Colonel Harland David Sanders (KFC)
Businessman. KFC Owner.
He wasn't able to sell his chicken. More than a thousand eateries turned him down.

Stephen King
American author of horror, supernatural fiction, suspense, and fantasy novels.
Carrie had thirty rejections for her first novel.

Soichiro Honda
Japanese engineer and industrialist. Established Honda Motor Co., Ltd.
He was turned over for an engineering position at Toyota, leaving him jobless.

J.K. Rowling
Writer.

While writing the first Harry Potter novel, she was unemployed, divorced, and raising a daughter. Twelve publishing houses turned down her manuscript "Harry Potter."

CHAPTER 30

Humility and Happiness

Being humble and finding happiness are two things which can be linked or not, depending on each person, but I wanted to unite them to give greater importance to being humble as an essential part of a human being. Everybody already knows that happiness is everything in life, and it is the greatest purpose to aspire to, but being humble is also important because it opens your mind to learn, ask, receive information, discuss and reflect on everything and most importantly, on yourself.

Humility is one of the foundations that make up the character of a person. There is a phrase that says "If you want to be arrogant, you have to be worth it"; but the truth is that nobody has to be arrogant when he/she succeeds because it does not lead to anything good. A person with knowledge and experience does not need to lose humility; indeed, the wiser you are, the humbler you have to be because it is precisely when you realize that you know nothing that you can always improve. A humble person does not need to prove anything to others, only to himself/herself.

The reality is that the size of a person's drama is proportional to the size of their ego. We don't need to be arrogant or to have an ego, and if we need it, it's because we have an inner problem that we must fix. Being humble is learned from those around you and from the context, and it is acquired with years of experience. A lack of humility is shown in many ways, for example, the need that many people have to speak badly of others to make themselves feel better; this indicates fear and no self-confidence in the one who does it. A confident person who knows who he/she is does not need to constantly tell what he/she is doing or what he/she has in life. If you are happy with who you are, you don't need to show anything to anyone, because you already know what you are worth.

As we discussed in previous chapters, the key is "to be or to appear". What is more important, to be or to appear?

"To be" - It is the essence of what we should be as human beings, working day by day for our goals regardless of what others may know about us. You want to make yourself and the world a better place every day, working hard regardless of whether people know it or not.

"To appear" - It is without a doubt to focus more on the environment and try to control what is perceived about yourself than to focus on you and what you really are. It happens when you want to show an image to others, instead of first worrying about being the best version of yourself.

Without a doubt, the first is the option that we must always choose. However, we are not going to be hypercritical, because the second has its importance in the twenty-first century as well. Unfortunately, in life, although we should be more interested in being, appearing is also important at times, because we live in a global world where what others think and say about you matters. So, being must prevail, whereas appearing can be of some importance when striving to attain higher goals.

This is seen often in football. There are many very good players who appear less than they are. There are many footballers with friends in the press who get that bit of extra coverage, and it helps to improve their image. Undoubtedly, good press is beneficial for you; it improves your public image and makes everyone look at you in a good light. On the other hand, that player who does not receive this "help" does not have his name on the lips of the people and has a worse image. This example, which has happened and will happen again, occurs in all sectors in one way or another. You have to know how to be the best version of yourself and also surround yourself well so that your social image is the best it can be. Everything helps, but remember, you should never cross the line of dignity and honour and you should never sell people or lie about others to win; doing that is equivalent to losing your values and we cannot ever lose those, because that would be the end of us as a person.

When one has reached that level of knowledge, experience and class that makes a person humble in their day-to-day life, that is when the tranquillity with himself/herself is complete and that is when "happiness" is felt; we do not often feel it, but when it arrives, it is special. Happiness comes with inner peace and the idea and feeling that life has a meaning and that you are getting everything you can get out of life; because that is what life consists of; in living it and in feeling that you are alive in every second.

Happiness depends on the relationship you have with yourself and what you are and want to be as a human being. You have to get away from the materialism that this world is focused on and get closer to yourself. It is said that as science progresses, the human being moves further away from God, but I think we are getting closer because once you analyse the good and bad things that are happening to you and you see that there is still a chance to find happiness despite the bad, you see that there is 'something' out there. Then you can approach God and find your peace and happiness within the world.

Once you know who you are, you are ready to live for real, which is the greatest level of courage that exists and not many people reach it. Being happy means knowing who you are, where you are and what you want; three big things but impossible to get if we ask ourselves the wrong questions. So, let's ask the right questions:

Am I improving my life every year?
Do I like what I am doing?
Do I like myself as a person?

Just ask these questions in order to be safe, relaxed and in good form with yourself, waking up every day knowing why you are in this world and what you are going to do for it. It is difficult to tell what makes people happy because we are all different and have different desires. Also, in this life, we should be aware of the fact that today, you could be on top of the happiness, and the next day, you could come down like a ton of bricks. Many situations and contexts can put you on this path or another, so we have to be aware of it and stay calm in any situation.

The most important lesson is to have a balance between the future, where you should be thinking about money, studying or following a career in any role, and the present, where you need to spend some quality time because we don't know what's going to happen, so we need to enjoy the life here and now. Living in the present is the time when you can feel happiness, but it only lasts for a moment and then it disappears. However, tranquillity remains and lasts forever, and that is what makes you live with your head held high every day of your life.

In football, it is the same; happiness comes with success but especially when you know that what you are achieving has come with a lot of effort and from the most absolute humility. Those feelings are special and will make you feel proud. That is why being humble and feeling happiness are related because humility puts you in a position where you can improve as a human being and from there, you can achieve happiness.

Extra comment/thought/feeling:
Pedro López

Eintracht Frankfurt Scouter. Former Club Atlético de Madrid, Getafe CF, Real Madrid Castilla CF.

BEING HUMBLE IN THE PROFESSIONAL FIELD

This comes in accepting our own limitations and mistakes responsibly, while valuing our achievements from the eyes of HUMILITY with modesty and integrity, without boasting about them, and recognizing the role of others in reaching these achievements.

It is one of the best attributes that can be had and is necessary to succeed because it depends on being able to improve and also creating strong relationships with people around you. Everything is interrelated.

Another positive side effect of having a humble attitude towards life and taking it to the professional sphere is self-criticism. By knowing our own limitations but also our capabilities, we are able to stop pointing out to others and begin to examine what we have been doing wrong or not doing, which entails assuming our responsibility, but it can also be the key that opens the door to self-improvement and better professional development.

CHAPTER 31

Skills vs Surrounders

The ability of oneself to achieve his/her own goals by his/her effort is undoubtedly the basis of any professional career, but it is no less true that contacts are sometimes even more important. The first thing is your skills, which are based on a lot of personal effort made to achieve them, but then, we need the context to be favourable to be able to use our skills properly and in a good role.

Since we were young, the people who love us have always taught us the importance of work and personal effort in achieving our goals. It is a hundred percent real because with this mentality, you can get anywhere you want, but they don't teach us how important it is to know people or to know how to use our influence. All of it just to be in the right place at the right time, which is the key to success for any professional.

How much can our contacts influence our professional careers?

If you have done your part, which is to put all the effort and work into the plan to achieve your goal, now comes the part where all help is good. A contact at a key moment will help you to improve your image or even place yourself in a privileged position, because, as we said before, being in the right place at the right time is key. Contacts and influences are earned through personality, but also through actions that you carry out in favour of others, either helping them or doing something well on a personal level. You have to understand that life is made up of social relations and even with protocols and norms, the human part will always be there. If you like someone better than another, you will always take them more into account than the other; this is something simple and human and that will never change.

The same thing happens in football. Normally, the best player plays, the best coach is the one who gets the position of coach, or the best manager runs the club. However, this is not always the case, because it does not always depend on your skills but on the relationships you manage and what you can offer to them in terms of trust. Your personality also has an effect; no matter how good a professional you are, if you are not empathetic and open, you will see people who will prefer someone worse at what they do but more open and with "social skills" to run their business.

At any level, having a good relationship with people, showing a positive attitude, giving an image of seriousness and knowing when it is a good time for joking and when not, etc., may seem trivial to some people but they are very important for the people who control the business because they only want trustworthy, positive and professional people, who have a great deal of common sense, running their business.

Therefore, we continue with the message that your skills will be the key to your success, but surrounding yourself with good friends and managing social relationships will be what takes you from a medium role to being able to have a top role at any level in any type of structure or company.

How do you improve your social relationships?

Have an opinion, respect the opinions of others and be serious and empathic with their problems. Show joy and tranquillity, alongside the desire to help and collaborate. Helping people opens doors for you because they see that you are trustworthy. Give your best and offer support to both those who follow you and those who cannot. Try to be calm and balanced in your life, which is a good image. Have knowledge but know when to speak and give opinions, because the moment to say something must be right and we need to distinguish between good and bad moments for each situation. Appear educated and a joker at the right time and when the situation is right. You have to know when to talk about serious issues or when to joke, when to talk about a family anecdote or when you can tell something about work. You don't have to do anything special, just be open-minded and normal in your actions, and know when your time has come.

All these things help; you don't have to have a plan, but understanding every situation in life is key. Always stick with your truth but respect others, debate and be open-minded, and be kind and committed while remaining calm and emitting good feelings. Show a good combination of personal effort and context management. Also, the relationships with the people that make up that context will be key for you to achieve your goals. You have to know how to play without crossing the lines but being intelligent and using things to your advantage.

We've talked about the importance of trust. It is vital that people trust you in order to give you responsibilities, but as we said in previous chapters, we cannot trust just anyone in life, only a few people, so it is a very difficult thing to predict or control. Often, we get on with some and not so well with others; there seems no reason for this other than a feeling. Therefore, the luck factor, the factor of meeting people related to you or not is key, but we cannot control it. What I can control is what depends on me. There are no recipes to succeed or not, but there is a way of behaving that can serve you, and that is what I have tried to explain in this book.

It is a fact that you can be good and have skills in a specific matter but if you don't have good and professional people around you, you will go straight into a hole, because this life is about being social, about contacts and about trust. So, try to recognise the people we can trust and the ones who only come around when they want something. Remember that if you have dealings with bad people, you will become one of them as well, so, here is a quick guide to help you: Believe in the people who give without asking, work without complaint and the people that have skills and show those skills every single day; those people will be good for you as friends and as professionals.

Common sense is the most important skill that you could have in this world because it affects how you see the world and how you adapt it to your benefit. We need to know how to analyse everything, but if we do not succeed, it is not a problem – let's just try to improve it next time.

To sum up, develop your skills as a professional and a person; try to find good people to share this life with; if not, it's always better to be alone than to share life with bad people. It is a tough life that we live - social media has taken our privacy away, and the world will never be as it was, where you could judge people face to face. Now, the world is as competitive as it was, but we still call the people on Facebook friends. It is a world of madness and the only option to be happy is to use common sense to benefit us. Improve every day, surround yourself well and you will succeed, in one way or another, because sometimes, money is not everything, but living a good and calm life is. Football is exactly this, show what you are worth and be smart to boost your victories, improve and reach your goals.

Extra comment/thought/feeling:
Deshi Bhaktawer
South African TV Football analyst. Football coach in the Premier League of South Africa and the Indian Super League.

It's important to remember that even an inborn talent has to be nurtured and developed. I believe that most sports people are aware of the hard work and many lonely hours spent working on your career. Most even understand that this work does not stop throughout a career; there is always a constant striving for improved performances. Within this development, there are lots of intricacies which form part of the development of a career.

Contacts which we make along the way are vitally important in the growing of a career. Even the most innocuous meeting could, somewhere along the line, play an important role in growing one's career. It is important to note and remember that it is human nature for one to feel important and to be given attention. Therefore, whoever we meet, it is important to treat them with respect, compassion, sincerity and honesty. Some of these relationships are going to need nurturing and looking after for many years to come. Also, keep in mind that a fleeting meeting could, years later, prove beneficial in a career if this seemingly casual meeting made an impression. The development and growth of a career require lots of assistance, help and support throughout.

CHAPTER 32

Gratitude

Life is composed of gratitude towards itself and towards the people who really love you, and those are the people and moments that you will take with you when you disappear from this world. Be grateful to those who helped you and who still help you day by day. Sometimes we do not realize it, especially when we are young with our parents, or sometimes it must take time for us to realize who was really with us, supporting and who was not.

In football, you will see just a few people who help you without wanting something in return, because it's not very normal. This can be caused by exchanging favours, knowledge and contacts in an attempt to keep everyone equal.

As we said in previous chapters, "As you sow, so shall you reap", and these are keywords to understand how to behave with the people around us. We will have many bad moments where we will be deceived and where there are people who will disappoint us, but we must keep trying to generate those synergies and continue to be open and grateful to the good people with whom we share life. Sowing is giving; giving before expecting to be given to you. This mentality is the correct one, although not everyone deserves it and we must be very careful with the people with whom we share our time, and especially to whom we give our trust.

Being grateful comes mostly from realizing what we have. If you were born in a rich country, even if you were not born into a rich family, you will always have the chance of having a good life, but it depends on you. You must analyse how lucky you are and take advantage of it. Realizing the environment and the possibilities you have with respect to others should make you smile and fight for your goals.

Being grateful can be shown with actions rather than words; it is in the day-to-day where we show how much we love our people, how much we want something, etc. Everything else is just excuses. As a player, this is easy because you always have to offer your effort first and wait until you receive what you have earned. It may take a while, but in the end, gratitude will be shown. There can be no need for words at all as the effort speaks for itself.

Being grateful for what we are given and what we have is the key to good health, both mental and spiritual. We have to find those people who really gave and risked something for us, because they are who really love us, and we must be grateful. To know and feel that someone loves you is difficult and it must be said that if in one life, you manage to have three or four true friends, you must be happy as true friends are very hard to find.

Sit down and close your eyes for a moment and think about the world in which we live and the problems that torment us. Then, think that depending on the age and luck you have, we will all die in a number of years, ourselves and the people we love. Ask yourself if it is worth wasting time on nonsense.

Doesn't it make you think of being a better person and enjoying and being grateful for what you have?

We have to make sure that our life has a meaning for us and for the people we choose to share it. To say thanks for the life we have means to value it, love it and most importantly, respect the people who love us. It's not an easy thing to live in a world where things are changing so quickly. Social media has changed how we live, just like the TV did years ago, but we have lost our privacy and people don't care about it. We have all changed; it's a fact but we need to find ourselves and get the stuff we really desire. To be happy and to enjoy our happiness should be the first consideration. Sometimes we are obsessed with stupid things or invented problems, which make no sense, and we forget what it is to really live, to love those who love us and to do what we want.

In football and in life, there are always people who transmit negativity, using the "If only…". No one should tell you how good you could have been, so make your decisions and be happy with what you have lived and follow your path. The only thing impossible to change is your death; everything else has a solution and you must appreciate every day you have in this world.

To say thanks means to be at peace with yourself; it's a great feeling and you have to be proud of yourself first. Being proud depends on us, and how we live our lives. Life can be easy and difficult at the same time, so just keep the balance and have a healthy life. Work but also rest; have a good active social life but spend time just talking to yourself. Stop and listen to what surrounds you because sometimes, by listening, you can find peace or identify what you need to change. Feel and transmit those feelings to others because we are all connected, and live as if it were your last day.

Be grateful for what you have every day, smile, and be good to others. Every day could be your last and we are always worried about nonsense and things that are not on the same level as life. Life is spending time with your parents, going to dinner with your partner, training with your teammates, enjoying a trip or a game, and all that effort that involves but, at the same time, it gives you happiness and you are alive. Take advantage of the time and fill the bag of life with experiences, because that is why we are here, to live it and enjoy everything that happens to us.

APPRECIATING – THANKING – LOVING – FEELING

Extra comment/thought/feeling:
Life is beautiful when you know that it may be your last day. Have the ability to give thanks for what you have and the energy to fight for what you don't have but still want.

CHAPTER 33

Escape

There are times along the way when we need to escape. We feel we need a change but we don't know how to do it. Doubts invade our life and although it is difficult, we need to change because we are beginning to lose time in life; we have lost all faith in the present.

Sometimes, routine terminates our creativity, the will to live, and the smile that we should have. Sometimes it is not the routine, but the context in which we are and we cannot face it anymore. All this creates stress that, in the end, cannot be borne. It's like an injury that begins with discomfort, a discussion with the coach not analysed and resolved later, or like any problem that is not solved and becomes bigger.

Sometimes, it is good to escape because we need to be alone to think about life, however, most people cannot bear to be alone. Yet, it is a fundamental part of life to escape and to be able to talk to yourself; it makes you a better human and lets you know yourself in a deeper way. Sometimes the answers do not come out because we do not ask the right questions. We should ask questions even if they hurt us, so do not hide with excuses or remorse; we have to be clear with ourselves and open our hearts totally. To lie to oneself is not a good thing to do because you are your best friend. You have to live with yourself every day and improving or not is up to you.

People being wary of facing their own fears prevents them from leaving their comfort zone; they are comfortable there and they feel safe in a world they hate. Their desires remain unfulfilled and they do not get what they really want. This is due to multiple reasons, but the greatest is the social pressure that we have to follow an established lifestyle, marked by the brands, governments and classes that make us comfortable and which conform with what we have, even if we don't like it. Once we have the courage to escape from the ties that stop us living our life, we will be closer to happiness and inner peace. To really know oneself means to be totally open and this requires a lot of courage.

Above all, we have to understand that we need freedom. A full life is never achieved without a clear sense of freedom. If we feel that we have lost it, it can seriously affect our life and performance in all areas. We have to take care of ourselves on a psychological level and take breaks that help our body and mind to reset in order to continue fighting and staying focused on the goal. The same thing happens in football - we may need to change clubs, but we have to do it positively and with a calm mind. Have a Plan B and do your homework about the positive and negative things that you may win or lose by choosing one path or another. Nothing should be left to free will; we must always have everything under control, or at least try.

The first thing we have to work on is our life plan. Having a good balance between work and social life allows you to have a good physical and mental balance. We also need breaks that avoid monotony and combat fatigue. Your life is more important than anything else because what we gain one day by expanding our efforts may be lost tomorrow as we cannot offer more effort. Despite doing everything we have to, the day may come when we have to change our life professionally or personally. It can happen, but we must always have a plan according to the level we want to have in life, and the level is demonstrated with an organized plan and daily effort.

There are many times in life that even with a good and happy life, the situation can destroy us for many reasons. A bad situation can cause a loss of love on a day-to-day basis, and that's why we must be psychologically prepared to do what we must do, accept what we can change and be courageous to make the changes that are necessary. However, it is never advisable to change from one day to the next, and we should never make changes at a time when we are not calm; coming home, relaxing and thinking calmly is the key to organizing the plan. In football, decision-making is constant and many times we find ourselves in a bad moment where we want to change. We have to do it calmly and with a plan; for example, when signing for a club. There are many concepts to think about and discover before signing.

We are going to start by analysing the general view of your job as a footballer. We must know the league and the type of league it is in terms of game speed, level, the level of your team and whether it is suitable for your goals. You also have to analyse the competition to your position in the team, what the coach thinks of you, contractual questions, questions related to the context of the club or the league, etc. Consider questions like: Have I been a signing of the coach or the management? Are there more players in my position? Do I know someone in the press? What salary do I have compared to the rest? etc.

In contractual terms, you have to analyse years of contract, bonuses for each goal achieved and the salary and know at what point the club is in terms of financial stability, such as the league and federation. The contract must be signed by both parties, FIFA and the club, and in addition, registered in social security, etc. We just need to control all factors. If you are moving to a foreign club, because in football you are not going to be spending too many hours training, it is important to know the country and its culture, the city/town where you are going and find out about the people, languages and history and then you have to adapt to the setting. When you work in another country, it is not the country that should adapt to you, but the other way around. All the aspects are related and share synergies, but they must be treated in a specific way and with the greatest specificity so that it is as professional as possible.

All this creates a sense of control in your life, which can be helpful in avoiding falling into depression or wanting to leave everything. So, although changes are sometimes necessary, we must always try to control what we can in terms of our personal and professional life.

There will probably be times when you feel that you have finished one stage, and you have to follow the path elsewhere. When you know that the moment has come, move on using your plan and have courage. To have a plan and trust your capacities is the key to achieving your goal. How you react to the bad moments and how you deal with the problems are always important. In this life, problems come and go but how you deal with them means everything; moreover, it affects your personality and how you manage your life in terms of happiness.

To be happy should be the final goal that we all must have but how to get there is the question. My advice here is to have Plans A, B And C; focus on the things that you like, but be smart in the environment in which you live; always be open-minded in terms of adaptability. Also, find the right people for you to have as close contacts – friends, partners, etc. That is the key to getting what you want because we help each other and that is the basis of life. However, if you are not happy, there is always a way out, so plan for it and go for the next challenge. Nothing and no one should stop you; sometimes "escape", to change, is the only solution.

Extra comment/thought/feeling:
It is normal to have a desire for things, to want things, to want to do things, but we need fewer things than we think.

CHAPTER 34

Sport "Circus"

Sport is a healthy, playful activity that has been used at an educational level for many years, but also as a transmitter of values or as a control of certain feelings and/or attitudes of society. It has even been used as a form of distraction to draw people away from their problems.

Why does the title of the chapter have the word "circus" in it?

The Roman "circus" was created in its day to entertain the social masses, and when you have people entertained by something, they may momentarily forget about other things that may be happening in society. Football as a circus is a very powerful weapon and exerts control over people; indirect control, but control nevertheless. It is a simple but very effective way to distract people's attention and it works.

The Romans controlled the people in a way that was not very different from now, and once a year, they prepared the Roman circus with gladiators and different fights and exhibitions to entertain the crowd. The aim of these games was to distract the people from the fact that the emperor had an amazing life and the people didn't have any reason to be happy in those years of misery, so, they opened the circus, and, for a couple of weeks, the people forgot about their real life.

Football has the same effect on people today. People are not so inclined to get together to protest about politics, governments and their bad management, but when a football club gets relegated or disappears, everyone comes together to protest and fight for their "colours".

How can we explain it? It does not make any sense that the crowd should protest more over the relegation of a football club than the high rate of unemployment, for example.

The reality is that this is only one of the many things that are used to keep people in check or entertained; it is nothing new. Loving football is good, but let's not forget what happens in the world, the important things to fight for, for a better life. But this is the reason why sports or other distractions are so important for governments because they are a great way to stop people from thinking about the real problems the country may have. This may sound harsh to some, but it is true and we should be aware of it.

It should also be noted that human beings have a natural need for effort and competition against others. However, we can be grateful that nowadays, sport is reserved for competition and there is no violence involved.

Why should I know these things?

As football professionals at any level, you have to understand the business thoroughly, and from there, focus on what you have to do, but always keep in mind where it comes from, where it can go and its positive and negative aspects.

The circus is created to be profitable, which is normal and good because nothing is built if it does not generate a return. We must accept our role within the business, in your case as players, but, at the same time, in the service of the club. We also have to acknowledge all the different local, national and international associations, the leagues and especially the markets. The markets control everything because they negotiate television rights, which are the ones that control football because they are one of the sources that generate the most money. Yet, the more global football is, the better for us, because with the synergies between countries and markets, everything goes from being local to global, which makes the business grow.

The word "business" should not scare us; nor should we use it as something negative because, as we said before, every sector needs some returns since nothing is done for free. So, once you remove this misconception from your mind, we have to understand that business is key and we need to keep fighting to get the best possible working conditions for us. The life of a footballer is short and we cannot simply let the years float by. However, it is not good to be too ambitious, because, in general, excessive ambition is bad. As we always say, aim for a good balance between salary, life and your goals. When it comes to understanding business, it is important to have someone who takes care of legal issues, offers advice and takes care of you because then, decisions can be made calmly.

We must always be careful with the context. For example, it is good to have an open relationship with members of the press, but not too open. Remember the sentence; "You only own what you do not tell anyone"? Never tell all your thoughts to others because many will use them against you. There are many people in football who will lie to hurt you and take some benefit, so concentrate on always doing your job and go head-on with your bosses. With other people, be careful and distinguish between those who can be trusted and those who cannot.

Understanding and controlling your environment is the key to success, and people who lack this are always the ones who fall. Listen, see and remain silent, analysing where you are, your surroundings, your goals and the people around you; that is the key to success. Listen more than you speak and speak only when necessary, and do the same with your thoughts. Have friends, but real ones. This simply requires a mentality focused on you and your goal, and not letting anyone intrude on it, for they will try if you give them the slightest chance.

Your relationship with staff and management must remain professional. Try not to mix business with pleasure, but if a friendship arises, do not be fooled into thinking that by being a friend of the Board today, they will extend your contract tomorrow. The only thing that matters in this business is the present, as the past is forgotten very quickly and we must adapt to it, understand it and play it to our advantage. A football club seems very big, but that's for fans; professionals know how small it is and every gesture and comment is scrutinized. This doesn't mean you should be stressed over it – just recognise it and understand the context you are in.

At a general level, it is good for the business and ourselves that football is increasingly global and expanding to more places. This indirectly benefits us because it gives you the possibility of playing in your country, being able to play in another and having many varied experiences. Also, you have to take advantage of time; the professional career of a footballer lasts for a short time, and so does life itself, so do not waste a second – fill your spare time with studies and experiences.

With patience and working and adapting to the environment already created in the sector, we will always have the option to maintain ourselves in the business. Staying in business is often the difficult thing, as players first and then in any other branch or position. The sector has a structure that is difficult to change, and, at some point, it will be difficult for us to "love" the way things are done. Adapting and then trying to change things can only be done from the inside, and this is key to achieving your goals one step at a time. Remember that this is a wonderful business despite its ups and downs.

Extra comment/thought/feeling:
Do not believe everything you read or hear; manipulation is everywhere. Think for yourself. Have the courage to analyse everything and yourself coldly and honestly.

CHAPTER 35

Sports in the Community

Football as a sport reaches many people and can be a transmitter of values and principles, good and bad. The most important players, clubs and organizations have the power granted by the global audience that this sport has and therefore, the devotion of millions of people who "live and breathe" football. This power must be managed and controlled, so that it is always used in favour of the business, but also as a benefit for society and citizens.

Sport and football have an amazing power to unite people who speak different languages, who think differently, who live differently and who may even hate each other for their religious beliefs. We must take advantage of this possibility to truly create a better world for people and also to create synergies that serve to open borders and create businesses on an international scale, which would give people work opportunities.

Can we from football or as professionals help our community?

Yes, you can help. Children follow their idols and the organizations they represent, so you as a football player must represent your club and your profession with respect and your standards must be high, because you have a responsibility to carry the shield you wear and work hard, representing your city, your neighbourhood and your community. We should take pride in working where we work, feeling what we feel and representing what we stand for and this should never make us nervous or worried.

We have a great responsibility to teach and to be the mirror where others look to achieve their dreams. Think that a few years ago, you were the one who was 'there'; it is very important not to forget where we come from. Sometimes, we don't realize the good we do when we help someone, or when we stop walking to talk to a person who needs support. We must look beyond, and think that this is life because nothing matters more than helping and creating good synergies between people; that's the meaning of life and the community. Sports and football can save many lives and create visions for many young people, and cause a big impact in order to help them in their lives.

It is not only what football transmits, but it is also a link between cultures, where people of different beliefs can have fun together in the same game, without worrying about their country of origin, their religion or political thought. There is nothing better than sport for that and football is a clear reflection of this and its power. There are many clear examples at the community level where a good campaign or action can change the lives of many people, especially in uniting neighbourhoods where people are from different backgrounds, beliefs and cultures.

Due to the respect and devotion that football has earned over the years, it has enabled the development of local businesses, contributing to them becoming both national and global.

How to be a good role model for others and make a difference.

Being a role model is demonstrated day by day by your actions. As players or professionals in the sector, we have the obligation to show our best version, and lead the transmission of good behaviour, because we are instrumental in the education of many children, and, as we have previously discussed, acquiring knowledge through education lets you manage any type of situation.

Governments, associations, clubs and members of staff can contribute as well; all the actions that are carried out in districts, such as leagues, tournaments and other actions, where foundations and charities have a fundamental role, serve and contribute to the opening of communities. The problem that many neighbourhoods have is to teach young people that there is more to life than what they see there. Young people should know two things: Firstly, the world is very big and their neighbourhood is tiny in comparison. Secondly, in life, you can do whatever you want and progress however you want; it depends on you. If we can open their minds in this way, it will be wonderful.

From our position, we must promote these actions and be part of them. Helping others should be part of our personality, and we should be willing to put ourselves in the shoes of others with problems. Football is great for this because, with a ball and four stones to make two goals, people can improve their communication, forget the barriers, and can have fun and interact together in a game. It is something so primary that it shows us how easy it is to make people happy if good actions are promoted along with human values.

The dreams that you had when you were young are now those that others have, and we have the responsibility to show them the way. That is why one should take pride in being part of football, and consequently, being able to help and be that reference for so many young people.

Many times, although we come from different backgrounds where we have been taught about the world and life, we believe that others should know the same as us. You have to understand that some people are ignorant because no one has cared about them and they have no one to rely on and that is why they need us. We always talk about transmitting happiness and then getting it back from people. Thus, the poorest neighbourhoods need us, and those children need us; they need to know the world and we are the best ones to teach it to them. Sometimes, it's a moment that changes your life, a single instant that makes the difference.

Extra comment/thought/feeling:
Alf Brown
Member of The London Football Association Council, The LFA North East Division and The LFA Cups Committee.

Football and sports are to be considered as the most powerful weapons we possess in the fight against child obesity... Fact.

My years of voluntary youth work, which have included teaching at some primary and high schools spanning nearly 5 decades, have identified how imperative it is for any country to have an active and comprehensive sporting programme as an integral part of their national curriculum.

Everything must begin in schools because it is the only starting place where we, as qualified coaches, can influence, empower and inspire children to excel by simply utilizing sport as a conduit in their learning and development. But my experience has found that it is not only the children who require educating in the many attributes of sport; it is also their parents, the head teachers, the education boards and even the residing government. This paragraph alone is embarrassing for those in sole charge of education.

An education comprising of mental and physical study is a guaranteed way to ensure we produce a well-balanced child irrespective of their individual ability, and, in truth, should be a God-given right that adults/parents are 'contracted' to provide for every child.

By doing so, we are investing in our nation's children who will grow to have a balanced passive (classroom) and active (sports) education, with sports being the vital component encompassing the following: social skills, teamwork, personal well-being, equality, diversity, inclusion, discipline, tolerance, fun play and respect; all of which are basic human rights.

As a boy growing up in the capital city of London, I fell in love with this beautiful (bootiful) game, and would naturally play football with family, friends and even strangers who just wanted a game, one that could continue even when the street lights came on because that was our version of floodlit football. I also attended pro games to watch my TV heroes live, and the songs along with the atmosphere were awesome, win, lose or draw.

Having lived, studied and worked abroad, a desire to be a qualified coach began by becoming FA licensed in football, a referee, and also a basketball coach, with the sincere intention of helping "non-academy" kids get into team sports, and primarily, football. In order to do so, a community sports group called "Y2K" was formed to provide free, safe, fun sporting programmes during the school holidays.

My tenure as a member of the London FA council was my way of putting even more back into the diverse youth and adult communities I have served with honours and distinction for over 45 years. So, personally, from a 25+ year financial background, encompassing playing semi-pro football and organising free sports tournaments in various London boroughs, I have run after-school football programmes, chaired/coached a girls/ladies club with honours, and the work continues to this day.

Therefore, in order to safeguard our beautiful game and ensure its nurtured growth at the 'real grassroots' levels, the "powers that be" need to give level 1 & 2 Coaches a voice at council and board level, as they are STILL volunteers, and the only volunteers who introduce our children to this exciting game. England's next Rooney, Bronze, Beckham or Kirkby will always come via our volunteers.

Also, at the individual level, professional players and ex-pros could also help, with agents and sponsors, by donating to fund 3/4G floodlit football training sessions, that we can ill afford. Football pitches that are akin to fields also need serious attention and should be free for registered teams. Essentially, the REAL grassroots game needs REAL backing/support from the over £4bn generated every pro season; yet we at 'grassroots' have been assured and promised for decades, but this has barely materialised in its trickle format.

In closing, the points made in all of the aforementioned were ALL made possible by one solitary person with no high profile, no abundance of finance; just a deep passion to see children from all or any background aspire to be happy by just simply playing sports, learning how to take care of their body, and being a team player. Our society needs team players if we are to survive as one race.

CHAPTER 36

Sports and the National Identity

Sport has been used throughout history for multiple purposes and in many ways both positively and negatively. Sport has replaced, on an emotional and even psychological level, the old battles or confrontations. Now, thank God, the civilized countries of the world fight each other in many ways, but not in a physical way, where sport has replaced that patriotic feeling of showing our "physical" superiority over other nations. Now, countries fight with the economy and markets, which are the ones that direct decisions, even political ones.

It is good to promote sport because it transmits values, that's why it is consolidated in education and it is essential for health. It is an industry where many people work and is very good as a facilitator of synergies, where many industries and businesses are nurtured. Sports, and especially sporting events, have the facility to bring nations, companies and other factors into the equation, in order to promote new business and relationships.

Sports and football are key for a country because they represent an image. Many times, it is not understood why countries want to celebrate a football event but they have an economic purpose because they attract investment, create synergies as we have already talked about, and above all, offer an image to the world. Even though there are issues going on in the background, a good image is key. However, it is important to be aware that not everything may be rosy. That awareness can ensure that no one uses you for a purpose that is not legitimate or where you do not make a profit. People will often try to use your image for a purpose that is not what they have told you, so you have to be smart not to get involved, or at least to make sure you get something back from your participation.

Therefore, for a young player like you who just wants to play, you should focus on that, but also know and understand that sport and football is a business, not just a game. If you want to understand this business that you are getting into, you have to go further and understand where we come from. As we said in a previous chapter, we come from the Roman circus; we come to offer the people a show with various purposes. One is that they have fun with a competition, especially physical, that satisfies the need that the human being has for confrontation, competition and fight. And then there are other purposes, such as distracting the people so that they forget what really matters, such as bad management of a country, for example. Also, sports victories can be used to generate relationships that benefit certain leaders on a personal level or to enrich certain people because power over the masses is the true power and is very useful.

With the positive and the negative, you have to understand that football moves people, emotions and feelings that go beyond love; it is a feeling of belonging to something. You may have lost your feelings for your country, but not for your football team. As a professional, you have to focus on being "professional", today, working for this club and tomorrow, with another. You cannot act like an amateur or a fan unless you are going to get something back, or you know that this club is where your future lies. Identifying with some "colours" can mark your career for better or for worse, so you have to be careful when speaking.

Moving a large social mass gives power, how to move it and with what interests is the key, and as players, you are going to attend situations where that social mass is lied to, where that affection is used and where somebody wants to direct your message in a certain way. The clubs and the press are united in everything. The press gets news because the clubs give it to them, as they want to send the message in one direction or another. This is how it works and this is how it will always work. As a player, and for your benefit, it is good to know how it works, in order to do your job on the pitch and off it.

What is work off the pitch?

You have to maintain a seriousness and values associated with work and commitment to your club, be professional with the management and staff, and maintain a certain closeness yet distance with the fans. Having friends in the press will be useful because information is power and they can speak well of you. You would be surprised at the number of players who have improved their careers because some journalist has made them look better for the public than they really were. Controlling the environment is what gives you power, considering you accessible and at the same time reserved, and never saying what you are thinking unless asked by a trusted person; information is power for good and for bad. Controlling your environment is key, be it through off-pitch relations with the management, contract timings, or links with members of the business for future deals. You need to know and understand how the club uses you to benefit itself, and in that way, you can negotiate your rights better with your club, with your brands, etc. Always have a good attitude towards everyone, but be smart and know how to organize what you have. You are your own boss, and you need the knowledge that we always talk about to avoid wasting time and money.

Controlling what happens in this business is the important thing. Of course, never use people, lie or betray anyone; that goes against the values that we have, and you will never see those things advocated in this book. Be smart and know the context to adapt to it, but as we have said before, never deceive or lie to anyone.

To conclude, we must talk about the greatest moment that a professional can experience, which is to represent your country. The feeling of belonging helps you in life to feel loved and encourages you to fight for something; for an ideal, values, for the family and your origins. It must be an honour to be able to represent your country, but also a challenge, because it will mean that you will be one of the best in your country, that among all the children who once dreamed of playing football, you have been able to be one of the best. You must admire these achievements and above all, know that we must always aspire to the maximum in order to at least be close to the target. The one that aspires to the minimum will not even reach that minimum. Setting ourselves high challenges helps us push ourselves and give the best we can. The greatest thing about football is that you can give your all, love your roots and your family and enjoy the effort, the honour and the fun of fighting for what one wants and enjoying the pathway through life.

Extra comment/thought/feeling:
Juan José San Román Milla
Currently at Al-Nasr FC. Former Head of the Academy of AD Alcorcón. Former Real Madrid CF, Club Atlético de Madrid.

In football, the environment you set matters. "The set of circumstances, social, cultural, moral, economic, professional, etc., that surround a thing or a person, community or time and influence their state or development."

In this case, I will not talk about moments of injury, of looking for references and examples within this discipline that is football and, in particular, professional football. I will try to be concise and draw something that should be very easy to carry and, from time to time, it becomes a real martyrdom.

- Do you remember that boy from school who was so good at playing football? What happened to him? -

- He did not "get it". He was not focused!

We have all known a player like that; a childhood friend or someone in your neighbourhood that everyone was talking about.

But when a player gets there?

Some football players turn professional and once they retire, they have nothing. How can it be?

The answers are as endless as situations and players exist.

But sometimes there are a number of common factors that trigger the bottom line.

This is not about blaming or denying responsibility - it is just going over a cause to which sometimes we do not pay much attention.

The environment of the professional footballer.

We always ask players, from their earliest age, to train well and to acquire habits that help them reach their personal goals.

We ask players to train properly physically, technically, tactically and psychologically. Let them not avoid their responsibilities. They should have humility, respect and generosity. Learn to work as a team. Say no to rushing and go step by step. Take care of their eating habits and do not neglect their rest. We ask that at sixteen they have the technical-tactical concepts of a professional, which will be improved with training and experience. We ask them to avoid situations that are unrelated to the position they are pursuing and that are not conducive to their performance.

We ask them for everything to fulfil the goal, the goal of being a professional.

But what about the environment of this young athlete? How have the fathers and mothers, brothers and sisters, grandmothers and grandfathers, uncles and aunts, cousins and agents, been shaped to accept the new life of this new professional footballer?

Let's not forget that the career of an eighteen-year-old professional football player may already have involved more than a decade, dedicated and focused, body and soul, to his/her goal of reaching the elite.

That is more than ten years of training in a discipline, which began as a game and has now become a way of life.

And his or her environment? What training does your environment have to control or direct your career beyond your blood or friendship roots?

He/she fulfilled his/her goal. Now help him/her live and enjoy his/her dream.

The fact is, the environment has an impact, but it does not have to be negative. There are environments where seeking professional advice is frowned upon. That is why we are not going to generalize; we will simply talk about those environments that end up becoming a problem for that professional. We are not saying that all environments are good or bad, but there are some that are healthier and help in the development of a player more than others.

Names of professional players come to mind, and when I ask what if they had been better advised or their environment had been good and professional, I wonder, would their careers have been very different?

In this case, I am not talking about decisions when choosing a new club, a renewal or the new sports brand that will promote him/her for the next fifteen years. We are talking about an environment that is often very flawed with distractions that prevent the player from being focused on his/her goal.

In my years of professional experience, I have seen very talented players with great qualities disappear from this business and I have observed how players of a much lower level made a place for themselves and clung to it because of how well-advised they were and through their work ethic.

Young and millionaires, with almost assured futures. If we look back and rescue an old interview from that U12 tournament where those players shone the first time, they said; "... I want to get to the first team of this, the club of my life, win titles and help my family ..."

And that, that romantic goal loaded with work, effort, persistence and perseverance, placed them in their new reality.

Just as support was a very important constant to reaching the goal, in this new moment, the help of those around him/her will be the key to him/her being able to maintain that level and even improve it.

Family - friends - agent. This triangle will be vital for their survival in a sector where hundreds of thousands of boys/girls are prepared daily to take their place when their level decreases minimally. This triangle is often not understood, does not hold up and does not identify how important it is for the athlete.

The environment instils the values and principles of that young start, a young start who became a reality because of their preparation and talent. They are the ones who sometimes emotionally control the player, and with it, his/her career and heritage without any preparation for it!

"Now, don't forget those who were there when you were nobody".

"Don't change now that you're famous".

"Don't forget your people from the neighbourhood ..."

These are comments that young athletes have undoubtedly heard on their way to glory.

It is not about pushing or throwing a negative message onto the player, nor is it about making him/her feel guilty over his/her successes, those that with so much effort he/she has managed to move forward. It consists of doing the opposite - pushing him/her for more through healthy ambition, helping him/her and supporting him/her on his/her path, a difficult path full of uncertainty, because this industry is a global business, and it is far removed from what they think it is.

A professional life may be controlled by family members who, "... think they know about this business because they played football or because who better than them to look after their son/daughter?"

You may have friends as personal advisers who plan dinners and parties four times a week enjoying what they haven't earned.

Parents may be angry at their son's/daughter's new contract and make them feel bad for leaving home.

Professional lives may carry not only the footballer's concerns but also the wishes and desires of everyone who believes they have any right over him/her.

The professional player, with his/her new economic status, changes his/her house, his/her car, his/her hairstyle, the way he/she dresses ... But does he/she change or choose a new one?

Why shouldn't that professional choose a new environment that doesn't "manipulate" his/her new life?

The career of a professional should not be controlled by people who only see the player as a solution; an environment that sees in him/her the solution to their problems.

Just as the player chose the best studs for a certain surface on the day of his/her test, just as he/she chose to take care of himself/herself and not commit excesses to achieve his/her professional successes, now he/she must choose the most professional for the continuity of his/her career.

We are not talking about a total abandonment of all his/her surroundings. We are talking about everything that you detect that does not help you, and if so, and you manage to detect it, what has changed?

Big stars keep the same things that surrounded them since they were children and it works; although they also add people, they are professionals who really help them.

The environment must help, protect and support, and always think about development, which is the key to the player, a player who must learn from everything, to be the one who controls his/her own things.

There are environments that decide contracts, that advise against destinations, that decide shirt numbers... It is true that the athlete has the last word, but sometimes that player carries an "emotional backpack" that is difficult to leave behind. Sometimes, even the backpacks become very real and heavy suitcases from that environment that move with him/her to the new city of his/her new club and, instead of helping to adapt, they greatly complicate the new reality.

I know few professions where the new contract in the new destination adds a house and a paid car, and that your associates, who moved with you to make the "landing" more bearable, decided that the large house that the club offered you, near the training facilities, is very far from the outskirts and is not comfortable for them. What better way than for the club to keep paying for a central and luxurious five-star hotel in the capital for you, your cousin and your three childhood friends, without thinking the slightest bit about the image and impact it has on you and how those details speak of you as a professional?

While you run, take care of your diet, the recovery of injuries, and pressure yourself to perform better, and while the footballer tries to enjoy his/her childhood dream, his/her entourage, in this case very unproductive, dedicate their lives to living a dreamy existence thanks to your success – a rock star life for no effort on their part.

We have all ever wondered why football players marry and have three children by the age of twenty-two. I think it is simply due to the need for a stable environment that transmits peace of mind. It keeps them focused and helps in the continuity of their career and, although starting a family is not a surety of anything, it is the way sometimes to continue pursuing that dream for you and yours. It's the return to that interview from that U12 tournament ...

CHAPTER 37

Dreams and Mistakes

Dreams are the engine of life, where the first thoughts arise about what we want to be and achieve in our life. That first idea arises and, if we want, will become reality; it is always down to us. Everything starts with an idea, a thought and with time, a good plan and work, everything is achieved. It is the essence of life, dreaming about what we like and want to be, and what we aspire to in life on a personal and professional level.

Dreaming is free, but it is not enough, because we must make correct and adequate decisions at all times and for each situation; that is the complicated part of life. You also need a balance between what you want in life and what you must do to survive. It is not just a matter of the heart, as we spoke earlier; the mind is key. Mistakes are normal in life, but we must try to prevent them by good planning. Dreaming is a serious matter but we need dreams to make our life better. Having motivation is the key to a healthy life, but we should plan it properly. It is impossible to achieve a dream if we do not have the correct organization around us because we will not be able to make good decisions without order.

Dreams are the foundations we have because they come from the deepest part of us, from what we really feel and are passionate about. They are ageless because they can arise from when we are young or old. They are beautiful and always require an effort and some intermediate step, longer or less but that agonistic fighting effort. They represent the internal motivation that we have, which gives us the push to get up every day. Dreams can be very beautiful for the passion they generate but dangerous if it is not guided by the right path.

A dream must be protected and analysed to see its viability and then its execution planned for because nothing is impossible and if you really want something, it can be achieved. That is why we always talk about having to "protect" our dreams because we will have many people around us who will say that we cannot achieve them. They will tell you that because they are the ones who are not capable of achieving it. Envy, fear and the lack of motivation of many people cause these problems to arise. You will have to listen to those coherent messages that prevent you from making mistakes, but if you want something and it is analysed and planned properly, you must go and get it. Even if it means a lot of effort, you can get it; going for it is the only option because it is your life and what you live for.

As we have already said, balance must play a key role in life. Take a young footballer, for example. There are many players who, thinking that they are going to be professional footballers, do not want to study anymore, without understanding the concept of studying and what it will generate for their future. We are going to explain the keys to understand why they are wrong. The first thing is that a young player has time to do both, going to class and training, without any problem; they just need a good schedule. They have plenty of time to achieve it, plus, football training is just for a few hours a day, not like in other sports, so it's perfect. Secondly, even if we have a dream and we try our best, nobody guarantees one hundred percent that we will achieve it, yet education will always allow us to be something in life and to choose our path. Thirdly, even achieving the goal, we need to be educated because the more you earn and have, the more people will be around trying to steal and take advantage of you. Understanding and having knowledge is the key to knowing how to conserve, even invest and get a return on what you have already earned. Fourth and last, knowledge is the key to realizing yourself as a human being. What differentiates us from animals is the possibility of thinking, and being ignorant is the worst thing you can be in this life because you will always be directed and controlled by the context. So, studying gives you the possibility, whether you are a football player or not, to be independent in your life.

Errors are a key part of the process of achieving any dream or goal. Nobody is born educated and therefore, to err is normal and it's even logical and good that it occurs because it is when we learn the most, looking at ourselves without a filter, facing our problems and issues to improve. We must make mistakes to learn about life and about what we have to improve as a human because as a professional, we are always going to show what we are personally. We can separate many things but deep down, we are the same person at the personal and professional level.

Mistakes help us to learn because we can see the failure, analyse it and modify what we have done wrong. We are constantly learning, all our life, and understanding this is the key to continue growing. The only way not to learn from mistakes is to make excuses and blame others, which can be true sometimes, but we must try, even if that is the case, to analyse what we can improve ourselves, because it is the best that we will be able to get out of a mistake, failure or disappointment both personally and professionally. Therefore, the way to deal with a mistake is not by being defensive but, on the contrary, by being open-minded and realistic with yourself and your failures. That is the way to improve and it should be. In football and in life, everything happens for a reason and sometimes it seems that fate is made to fall and get up, fall and get up again.

In football, many mistakes are made by yourself and especially by not adapting to the situation. This word, "adaptation", is very important and will accompany us throughout our career and life, adapting to different contexts, such as colleagues, bosses, managers, environment, countries, clubs, fans, etc. Each place and situation is different and we have to adapt to what that environment requires, always with our values and morality as the foundation of our personality.

Error and adaptation are linked, since, once I have made a mistake and have learned, the process of adaptation to that situation or another similar is already internalized; it does not mean that I will not err again, but I will surely go in more prepared. As a footballer, I must learn from the things that happen to me, and learning and adapting is the key to winning on the pitch and especially off the pitch.

Be an honest person with yourself and analyze the environment before making decisions. Be willing to sacrifice everything for what you desire, but always have insurance behind you to guarantee a decent life if Plan A or B does not work out. Being happy depends on the balance that you got, and how you deal with success and failure.

You can get whatever you want, but you need to be ready to face ups and downs; that's life. If you really love something, you will go after it easily and, without doubt, you will get what you want. Take control of your life and organise a plan, then go for it; no fears, just believe in yourself but have a back-up and a Plan B and C. Life changes in two seconds and you will know what I mean, because that happens at work, in your personal life and in every single thing in our life.

DREAM - ANALYZE – PLAN - EFFORT – IMPROVE - ADAPTATION

Extra comment/thought/feeling:
Dreams are there, you just need to have the courage to go for them and pay the "taxes" because achieving your goals costs you in things like effort and sacrifice; it is how it is.

CHAPTER 38

Normality and Simplicity

Being a humble, calm, austere person in life requires having characteristics that come from knowledge, experience, and confidence in yourself. Being "normal" does not tell us much, because nobody can say what is more normal than something else, but we can differentiate between people of different characters and personalities.

People acquire a character that is defined by the context they have. It depends on them and their experiences, acquiring the maturity to be a real person and not someone who pretends to be something that they are not. As we said, each person understands the word "normal" differently, but in this book, being normal moves away from the eccentricity and chaos that many people like in their lives. It comes from the knowledge of oneself and the environment, from self-confidence and from personal and professional experiences in your country and others. It comes from the tranquillity and maturity of an independent adult without complexes or fears.

Normality and simplicity are keys to having a healthy mind, and entail a union of characteristics:

Experience + Knowledge + Clear targets + Self-confidence + Not needing to prove anything to anyone + Owe nothing to anyone

Sure, we can add more features, but these six would be the ones that would come out of common sense. They start with the experience

Normality and Simplicity

that life gives you, and the knowledge acquired that helps you to have clear objectives, and provides you with the self-confidence to know who you really are. Also, owing nothing to anyone and not having the need to prove anything to anyone, gives you the physical and spiritual freedom to be calm, and above all, to be able to do what you want when you want and how you want.

Experience is gained over time and with the sum of experiences. It is impossible to acquire experiences if we do not seek them. We have to go out into the world and open our minds to be able to learn. Being proactive and having the passion to learn and live is key; however, making mistakes is also an essential part of the learning process, as seen in the previous chapter.

Knowledge is acquired by those experiences and studying, listening, asking questions and having an open mind, always wanting to be with people who know more than you. Most people hang out with people worse than themselves, just because it makes them feel superior. But the person who is smart hangs out with people better than them in order to learn. You learn by listening more than talking, analysing and asking more than trying to appear something that you are not.

When you have those experiences and that knowledge, maturity comes and that's when we set ourselves clear objectives because we begin to know what we want. For all this, we need confidence in ourselves, but we acquire it along the way, during this process of maturation and learning. Self-confidence makes us love ourselves, to know what we can or can't do and what we have to improve because we have a clear picture of who we are. Knowing who we are and having respect for ourselves transmits security to the rest of the people and that is key in life. It does not mean that we do not have to keep improving; we have always to improve but from the security of what we are and our capacities.

Confidence in yourself is maybe the most important one and it depends on whether you have it or not. If you were born with it, empower it to improve. If you don't have it, we must work to reinforce what you think of yourself in order to get it, because self-confidence is necessary. For people to believe in you, you have to believe in yourself first; it is important to work to be good, but also to believe that you are good. For anything you do in life, having and showing tranquillity and control over yourself and the environment will offer you a world full of possibilities, where many people will open their arms to you because you give off a feeling of class and winning character, and that's what people like - winners.

The last two are also linked; owe nothing to anyone and there is no need to demonstrate your achievements to anyone either. We do not need to demonstrate what we are or what we want; we only have to demonstrate things to ourselves, not to anyone else. Regarding owing something to someone, there is no shame in helping or letting others help us, but we must try not to need anyone, because that is what makes us prouder of ourselves, and above all, allows us to be independent. However, it is a fact that synergies and teamwork are essential and necessary to be able to progress in life and in the world where we live.

As a footballer, you must do your job and be in your place. However, talking more than necessary and being noticed is useless because where you have to be noticed is in training, in games and when your team needs you to be a leader, contributing with your qualities. The true quality of a human being is knowing that he/she knows and not boasting, knowing that he/she can be bad but choosing to be good, being mature and probing it with actions, and using everything he/she knows for his/her good, for his/her people and the community.

Acquiring the characteristics discussed in this chapter depends solely on you and your desire to live, feel, work, love and suffer because life is a sum of everything and it is how beautiful it is. But always maintaining an air of calm, normality, simplicity and

Normality and Simplicity

austerity, whether you are very successful or not is what makes you a real human being and a true winner.

Extra comment/thought/feeling:
The important thing is the love of your people and the experiences that you live. Everything else disappears with time and death.

CHAPTER 39

Context

Context is everything, as it marks our life and sets the obstacles that we must jump to reach our daily objectives and goals, both work and personal. It is the thing that guides our way through the world, as our decisions are influenced by it directly or indirectly, whether we want to or not.

Talking about "context", we are talking about everything and nothing in the same word. It is everything because it is what surrounds us and unites us, what connects us with ourselves and with others. But, at the same time, it is nothing because we do not know what's going to happen or if we really can change our path, or whether it's all defined beforehand as many religious people think. However, no matter your outlook on this, we must adapt to the context, but also try to change it to our benefit and favour ourselves by improving ourselves and those around us.

Mastering the context will give you more control over your life and over the things that happen. We talk about directing what happens to you in a good or bad sense, but without controlling the context, it is impossible to achieve it.

Although we must try to manage our situation as much as possible, we must understand that no one has complete control over anything, and what is to happen will happen whether we want it to or not. Even with this, it is true that everything we do is to our advantage, and that is why we must be careful with the context and always try to mark our path. Besides, it is a reality that the harder you try, the better things usually turn out. It may take some time, but it will happen.

It is important to know how to adapt to the situation or try to change it which takes time and effort. How to change it is just down to us and our goals; but if you want to change it, you will do it. Being adaptable in life is the most important thing in all contexts and situations. We are talking about being able to commit and adapt to problems, changes, and situations that happen and only the people with this ability are capable of success.

We have to be clear about who we are and what we want and have a plan. Once we have a plan, we can adapt one step at a time. It seems easy but it is not; it requires effort, knowledge and, above all, patience and tranquillity. It is impossible to control your situation if you don't occasionally stop to think about what is happening and what your next step will be. Rush doesn't help; constancy does.

In football, the context is very wide. As a player, you have your team that is made up of your teammates, those you play with but also compete with for position, the staff who can help you or not, the management in the same line as the staff, your agent, and the other interests between clubs, associations and people involved in the business. It is a very difficult environment to handle even for star players who have a good, secured contract. My opinion has always been and will be, to focus on your work, earn your position on the pitch, and be smart off the pitch as well so that both you and your people are within the "circle of trust" that is important to you. Outside of that, do not get into problems that could make your relationship with the club become harmful to you.

Professional football is very tough, on and off the pitch. The contexts are interrelated and when they are interested, everyone wants something from you very quickly; when they are not interested, you are alone. You have to be mentally strong and choose the battles to fight, be professional and surround yourself well with people who protect you from things that may affect your profession. A football player should not worry about anything else other than playing, but the reality is that today's context is not the same as years before. Social networks make the world bigger but closer, and everyone can judge without knowing, and the news jumps from country to country very fast. To achieve your goal, control your comments, your actions, your relations and contexts and simply go step by step to reach your target.

It is important to know our context, but never use it as an excuse for not being successful. Remember that your success depends on you and not on your situation as it can be changed. What is important, though, is to have the knowledge of the context so that from there, you can focus on your objectives strongly and with conviction; the rest does not matter.

You have to understand that no one has bad luck in life. If you make an effort, there will always be a combination of good and bad things, so using the "lucky or not" as an ally will only calm your mind but not your soul, because deep inside, you will know the truth. Control your context as much as you can, have a plan and objectives, and work every day to get them, calmly but without pause. And most importantly, listen, see and keep quiet; one only owns what is kept to oneself.

The reality is that we will never be able to control the context, but knowing that it is there and it affects us is the first step. Secondly, knowing that sometimes we can get ahead of it and manage it in our favour, that's also true, but we have to be smart to be able to do that.

Let's divide the context into the things that you are going to experience on a personal and professional level. On the personal level, there will be two types of changes; family and friendships. At a family level, everything can change simply if you move to another city, or if you start to earn money. When you leave home, it pushes you to learn to be independent, because money does not solve everything; we must learn to do things by ourselves. Depending on your relationship with your parents, at first, you might struggle, but once stable, everything will go for the better because it is just one more step in life. At the level of friendship, we must try to maintain the good friendships that we already have and make others but never forget where we come from. A typical mistake that young people can make is that they befriend everyone when they go from having nothing to having resources or money. They also seem to want everything right now. Things happen in their own time and remember to save more than you spend, because everything could change in a second, just like the people around you. The context and what it brings with it should not change who we are, because the context will test us and we must have enough knowledge and control over ourselves to be successful in it.

Now that you are not in your usual neighbourhood, and you play for a football club and you have money, there will be many people who will approach you because of what you have and not because of who you are. Always keep in mind who you are and where you come from. No one should tell you that you have to change who you are or how you should live; it just takes time to work it out for yourself. What we need to do is understand that your situation has changed, so you need to analyse what you have, what you want and what your targets are so that you can adapt your lifestyle to achieve them. After all, good things take effort and time.

On a professional level, we are talking about a total change. You will be lucky if you always arrive at a football locker room and people welcome you. There are many occasions when it is like that, but not always because it is not a game anymore, it is a job where you compete with teammates to see who plays, and from there, you get more money or a better life. Work hard and stay away from problems. There will be problems – they are a part of life, but there is no need to push them to happen. Be careful with the people who control your career and money; we must understand everything so that nobody steals from us because it sometimes happens. Make use of the press and maintain a good relationship with them. After all, they are the ones who can promote you to fans who do not know you.

Control the environment, learn and understand what surrounds you, adapt and improve; these are the keys to life, to survival and even more, to success.

Extra comment/thought/feeling:
Eddie Munnelly
UEFA Licensed football coach. Former Tottenham Hotspur FC, QPR FC. Premier League Elite Coaches Scheme Award.

Making the jump.

The "TRAP DOOR" is one of the most difficult places to be in football. It's that place after Under-18s and 23s where the academy thinks you are ready and the first team brings you in but you are not playing any games for them; just training. It's when you get that rude awakening that even though you might train better than some of the experienced first team players and feel you can offer more than the players who are currently holding your starting shirt, you have ZERO GAMES and they have 200+ appearances and have played in World Cups/European Championships. Why would the manager drop this player, who has built up so much trust over his years and years of playing, to play you? You are 19 years old; you won't hit your peak for another 6 years. The average manager is in the job for 14 months, so why is he going to take a chance on you making your mistakes in his first team and that his 14 months end up being much shorter?

So, then your world shifts - you go from being the best player and starting most games to being the youngest player, being used for team shape in training whilst there are two games in a week and, at times, you maybe come on during the cups. This is the reality of most of the young professionals I work with/have worked with. This is if you are lucky!

98% of 16-18-year-olds offered scholarships at professional clubs are released or drop out of the game by the age of 21.

96% of players who signed a professional contract are either released or out of the game by the age of 25.

So, what is the solution? Consistency! Trust the process even when it seems like it is not processing…

Part of the problem is that a lot of these young players haven't really experienced enough failure during their young careers; it's all been too easy for them. So, when the first real barriers come, they do not have the coping mechanisms to deal with them. So firstly, from a development standpoint, as educators, we need to make our young players feel more uncomfortable during their developmental years. Then, when they experience discomfort in the future, it will not be so foreign to them.

Secondly, we need to help educate the young players to be emotionally intelligent and understand the world from the point of view of their first team manager. The young players need to earn their trust through doing the basic things extremely well day in, day out. At one of my former clubs, a 16-year-old was brought into the first team and compared to Messi by the first team manager. He was honestly one of the best young talents I have ever seen, however, not enough people around him were willing to tell him things he needed to hear rather than what they thought he wanted to hear. This led to complacency, poor body language, being poor in defensive transition and fashionably late or just on time to team meetings. He was quickly out of the first team and now, 7 years later, is just getting his career back on track in another country.

Another, with way less technical excellence on the ball, went on loan to a club in the second division and did not play a minute for this club's first team for the first month. The young man was dejected and felt like he wanted to end his loan and go back to his parent club. However, he took advice and trained like a beast day in, day out, interacted with all members of staff positively before and after training, was reliable with time-keeping and did the basic things extremely well every day - even when he did not feel like it. He did not play 1 minute for the team in 3 months then was asked back for pre-season. After that, he played every game in the league the following season. Having more appearances in the league than any other 19-year-old in his position, he earned trust and stayed focused on the process.

As a society, our Newtonian perception of reality conditions us to rely on and be governed by cause and effect; allowing external forces to control our behaviour/emotions. Players can fall into this trap and turn into a victim…blame culture is one of the most dangerous diseases in football… So, from my experience, the biggest indicator of success in young players making the jump has been their response to failure. Are they a victim or do they use every experience as a gift, no matter how badly it may be wrapped up, to grow/develop and move forward in order to achieve a version of their higher selves?

CHAPTER 40

Money

Money is the material reward for doing a professional job in any company. Apart from this obviousness, you have to see the role of money and how important it is both on a personal and moral level. Especially speaking of football and young people, we have to see the value that is given to money, and how it can affect the character and personality of a human being. Money can affect our personality, especially when we are young, and even more so if we have not received a good education that allows us to value things as we should.

This is a topic that is widely discussed by all kinds of people, both those who have a lot of money, and those who, on the other hand, have less money. Money is necessary to live, but we must focus the message on what money represents for a young person, and the changes it can cause in his/her personality and context because these will happen if they are not educated well enough to know how to handle the situation.

How can money affect a young person?

Money must be valued as a commodity that helps us to have a better life, but we must control the money, not let the money control us. There are many people, especially young people, and, in this case, young footballers, who are not mature enough and they have not got a good enough education to be able to handle money and the effects that can have on them. They just let money direct their life, change their personality and change their situation, and that of their friends, relationships and life in general. In the end and when the money runs out, all the benefits and the good use that could have been made of that money have been lost, and all those friends that they thought they had will leave them alone. Money attracts bad habits and bad company, false friends who would not be there if it were not for the money. In order to avoid making these mistakes, we must be well educated and become mature enough to surround ourselves with people who know more than us, being open-minded enough to always learn from them. We must understand that money is an asset that helps to achieve happiness, but money itself will not give you happiness.

What does money contribute to your life?

Money is essential for life. We work to earn money and to be able to be independent of others, but from there, considering other factors such as what we work for, what we live for and the profession we choose, what do these have to do with money?

What must be clear is that money does not deliver happiness, money provides "freedom" to do what we want and to be able to say "NO" to things. The freedom that money provides is priceless because it gives us the option to choose and discard options that we do not like or do not agree with, no matter the reason. We have to know how to use that freedom and the money to offer ourselves a better life.

People who believe that money brings direct happiness are the ones who believe in the accumulation of material possessions rather than valuing relationships, family and feelings. Material things make your life more comfortable and that causes or can cause happiness, but they are not the essential things. Those people who believe that money can bring them love, feeling and other sensations, will realize that they are wrong and, in the long run, it will cost them.

We must focus on how to organize our money to create a favourable context where we can set the foundations to have a good life. There is a popular sentence that says that "money comes and goes", so we have to try to make it come and organize it and invest it properly so that we can dedicate our time to what we like. As always, knowledge and values, in addition to asking and learning, will be key when managing and organizing what we earn. We don't have to know a lot about anything; just know a little bit of everything and be open-minded.

In addition, money cannot change who we are. Nothing material should change the way we behave in ourselves or with others. No one is better or worse for having more money or less, having a bigger or smaller house; the money may help to make your life better, but it doesn't make you better than anyone else. Again, education is the key to maturity and will distinguish the mature from the ignorant.

In football, it is normal that if you reach the elite early, you go from earning the minimum to earning a lot of money in a short time, and most importantly, "without any training on how to handle it". This is where the problem lies. It can be very easy for a 19-year-old earning millions of euros to let it affect his way of living and his actual personality because he has not received any training on how to manage the resources. Also, where before he only had four friends, now there are fifty. A poorly trained person will believe that those fifty people are there because they love and respect him/her for what they are. It is quite the opposite; people approach when they see success and move away when they do not see it. You will more easily identify the people who really love you in failure, not in success. It is very important to learn this because it will be key for your life.

Your personality as a human being, the way you relate to others and the way you live must be the same in all circumstances and with everybody, no matter what you have. Material things do not make us better; what makes us better are our daily actions. This is the truth about life and it should be taught at home and through the correct education. Young footballers need to have "teachers" by their side more than "coaches"; the word teacher encompasses more, and the player, as a student, must listen and learn.

From these values and considering money as an asset or means to achieve things, we can build a life that helps us achieve what we all want, which is happiness. Happiness is achieved from the tranquillity that knowledge gives you, control of the context, appreciation of the real people around you and the balance between all the things in your life.

Extra comment/thought/feeling:
Juan de Dios
Successful businessman, entrepreneur, and philanthropist.

From poverty, I keep humanity within me. From wealth, I kept humble gratitude. The road travelled has been difficult; I have been hungry, I have slept in the street, I have stolen, and all this has taught me not to forget where I come from. Today, thanks to effort, tenacity and God, my economic position has turned one hundred and eighty degrees, but I had a time when I wasted a lot of money and had friends who were not friends, but in the end, that was my education. Years have passed and life taught me that my best support was and are my values, values that were made and forged during the most difficult years of my life and that helped me when I went through the most difficult moments.

It is the values that will always accompany me, those that will always guide me along the path that I decided to take.

For guys who are into an elite sport and earn a lot of money in a short time, having never had it before, I would tell them to think that their professional lives can be short and fickle. No talent beats daily work and effort. I would give you an example; Balotelli, for me, clearly shows what can happen; it is a reality. Never lose your values and do not forget where you come from. Remember that work is the only way to be free and to have a life of your own, and it is up to you to be authentic or not.

CHAPTER 41

Desire vs Giving Up

Perseverance, sacrifice, the desire to achieve the goals we have or just the opposite, to quit. There are two types of characters, one with a strong personality that fights until the last moment, and the other type of people who quit because of the situation and for multiple life circumstances.

Where does the desire come from?

The desire to achieve things is intrinsic to the human being but everything requires effort and we also have a habit of trying to preserve the energy that we have and not waste it, which sometimes makes us lazy in making that effort necessary to achieve those goals. Everything comes from the inner desire to be something in life, to achieve things. This desire has made human beings reign in the world and be the dominant species. This spirit means we are not just living for sleeping, eating or having a family, but wanting to create things, discover, conquer, compete and dream big.

How do we handle this intrinsic double feeling?

The mind holds the key to everything in this life. Conviction, self-love, self-confidence and joy for living are the motives that we will have. It is our decision whether we use these, but there are people who do not want to make the effort or are afraid of achieving their dreams. The reality is that we can improve every day, create a better life for us and those around us and we can prepare our minds for this.

Success is found only in constant daily efforts rather than isolated bursts over a long time.

The same works in football - we need to work every day and even so, we do not know if we will achieve the goal, but we will only find out if we push our performance to the limit. As we said before, if we aim for the maximum, we may get there; if not, at least we will be close, but if the aspiration is just to reach the minimum, our performance will be poor. Great aspirations and hard work demand commitment from us, in life and in football, otherwise it will be impossible to achieve any goal.

Sometimes we will have the thought of giving up due to mental and physical fatigue, or lack of motivation that can often come from one's surroundings. It is impossible to be energized every day; there are always good days and bad ones. However, we cannot let circumstances beat us and we cannot make any decision without thinking it through properly and calmly.

Challenges happen every day in both life and football which is why we need trustworthy people we can rely on. Therefore, keep positive in your attitude and know exactly what you are doing and why – it's important to remind yourself from time to time. Life and football are endurance races; nothing is achieved in the short term; everything requires time and sacrifice.

Quitting is not an option. When we give up, it means that we have allowed what stands between us and our goal defeat us. If what we are doing does not make sense anymore, we are clearly exhausted and we have a desire to change our life, then we will have to do it, but that's not called giving up, just changing for the better. We have to distinguish between situations because they are not always the same.

We have to make the decision to go one way or another, and doubts will always arise, so what we think about ourselves and what we want are fundamental; these are the issues on which to base our strength as an individual. Everyone can reach targets if they want to, even those who are born with fewer capabilities than others – the effort involved, of course, is totally dependent on yourself and how much you are willing to commit. Often, the one who tries harder and is more consistent will surpass the one relying on talent alone.

Having a strong mentality is essential in life and for this, we have to be willing to let others teach us. A young person needs to listen and ask himself/herself questions and discuss the reasons behind it. This is the essence of life. There are many things behind making you complete and a strong human being and they include effort, understanding and a good education, but also being agile of mind and quick-witted.

Is it worth sacrificing your life for a dream?

We will always defend that on a professional level, we should never give up, but this comes with limits too, because there is a personal side too. We cannot base our whole life on work, but neither can we base it on having fun; a middle ground is the key. We all have to work and pursue our dreams, but at the same time, enjoy life, have a house, etc. That is a necessity to survive. On the other hand, not all of us need to have dreams and fight for them. In the end, it all depends on the targets and principles we have, and these are an essential part of achieving our happiness.

When it comes to prioritizing the things that are important to us, we have to look at the background to decide if we are making the right choices over the important things in life. Finding purposes to live is essential, but as we grow, our goals can change too. The negativity and agony of many situations make us lose all hope. But there is always hope and there is always time for self-criticism, thought and analysis which can lead us to change our lives.

We need our dreams to be real and not unrealistic and to know the difference. We also have to find the best balance between work, family and lifestyle to ensure we get the best from life. Then, when we find happiness, we will know that we have struck the right mix of doing what we want with people we love and with a lifestyle we deserve. Experiences, family and friends are going to be the best things that will happen in our life.

Extra comment/thought/feeling:
You never fail until you believe it yourself. You should never be discouraged by the negative things that happen because they are part of life and part of learning to succeed.

CHAPTER 42

Persistence and Determination

Each person is born with a series of skills and abilities in life. We have talked in previous chapters about many of these capabilities, some that require talent and others (the vast majority) that we have to get and improve with effort. Determination and persistence are two fundamental capacities that sustain our efforts because, without the ability to resist, to continue fighting despite adversity, we can lose everything we have previously gained. Moving towards the goal costs a lot of effort and the forward steps are short, but when it comes to losing, we can lose everything we have previously gained very quickly.

It all depends on how clear your perception is of the goals in your life. A life without professional and personal goals is empty, that's why we always talk about having a balance, and even more, we must always know the reasons for everything we do. We must build the foundations that support our path so, "the house" does not collapse at the first hurdle.

Sometimes, we ask ourselves questions like "What are we doing here? Where does the human race come from?" These questions have their place but don't spend too much time over them as they are questions without answers. Consider instead your awareness of what is happening in the world and leave these topics for speculation. We must choose a path and follow it even if it is sometimes difficult and these questions can act as a distraction if we let them.

The Things We Know and Do Not Say

Many times, it is through fear of failure that we prefer not to continue fighting. As a footballer, there are games in which everything goes well, but suddenly you miss a pass, you miss another, and in a few minutes, you are so collapsed, it is like being in "quicksand", that's why we must have a good mental balance so as not to fall into that. A real man/woman is not afraid to acknowledge their fears, because the key to overcoming a fear is to recognize it and adapt to it. In this way, we can resist what happens to ourselves without problems, because we are balanced as human beings.

Mental resistance is one of the things we need to have and improve; it will make us tough and able to resist the problems that happen in life because life is full of problems and new situations that arise. The human being in general always has the objective of controlling the environment, and it is not bad because the more you control, the better. However, we can never control everything.

The relationships between people and our situations can cause daily problems, so knowing how to be calm, confident and resistant to pressure situations is the key to success. By success, we are not talking about becoming millionaires, but about having a good life, doing a job we like, ultimately having peace on a personal and professional level, and in the end, achieving our goals.

How can we be resistant to what life gives us and takes from us?

Everything is achieved through our conviction in what we do and what we believe. We must understand our feelings and what we desire, in addition to the happiness that comes from working on what we believe. It is a balance between the heart and the mind, where we must always show common sense and responsibility.

As football professionals, we must isolate ourselves as much as we can from the negativity of the environment, from all the problems that are going to appear, and focus on talking on the pitch, in the gym, when we eat, and in every aspect of the life of a professional. It is the best way to resist physically and mentally, and not let things affect us. How problems affect us is more damaging than the problem itself.

Alone or accompanied?

In life, one can achieve success alone, but to stay and last, one must be accompanied. Relying on trusted people is the key to success. There are many people who believe that to reach the goal, it may be faster and more efficient if you are alone, but what matters more is staying there once you have reached that goal.

The key to persistence is knowing our situation, knowing where we are going, our goals, everything we've talked about that encompasses a life with personal and professional goals. Expressing feelings is good and necessary and keeping everything inside is harmful. No one has all the answers, so being able to have discussions with people in order to hear their opinions can open our minds and let us understand things that we would never have understood. Discussion is the basis of knowledge, listening to those who know and criticizing what surrounds us, always being humble and with a critical attitude towards learning, but never with arrogance.

Everything depends on you. If you want to achieve it, you can, you just have to create that balance and believe in yourself. We all have determination and perseverance, but you must have your mind and heart prepared to be brave and fight for what you want to achieve.

Extra comment/thought/feeling:
Failure does not exist, but the feeling of struggle, effort and personal improvement is real. If you want to be a winner, believe in it first.

CHAPTER 43

The Mind

The mind is the foundation where everything that we are and can be is based. It is the engine of our body and is involved in everything we do. There are many things that are important for a human being and we have talked about them, but the mind makes the difference between a winner and a loser because it is the part of us that directs what we do and what we can resist in life. Therefore, in this chapter, we are only going to emphasize what we have already seen, but it is important to dedicate a chapter to analysing the fundamental aspects that we need to understand about the mind in order to also improve it and make it stronger.

The mind guides our way and, when we have it prepared, makes us resist and keep fighting. We must be aware of how important it is to be healthy in mind, have clarity of ideas and know the environment to carry out day-to-day tasks. Our mind is everything; it is what pushes us to do or not to do, it is what manages our feelings, how we face problems and our happy moments; it is our engine. When we refer to a car and we talk about the engine, we are talking about what gives it the energy to accelerate the entire "chassis" which is our body and our soul. For the human being, it is the mind that gives us our energy, where we base all the effort that we need to deliver in order to achieve our goals.

Therefore, when we speak of having a healthy mind, we need to both use it and take care of it, referring back to the balance of which we have already spoken. This balance is supported by three pillars - emotional stability, confidence in ourselves and control over our context and decisions. These things are important for our balance and will provide us with stability in our present, and tranquillity in our future. In short, it is the calm necessary to be happy and content with our life. The key is to have a balanced life and that if something bad happens, not to lose our way or motivation, because our minds will be supported by solid foundations.

Achieving a healthy mind depends on us and our environment, and how we deal with several factors such as work, family, partners, property and possessions, etc., everything that makes us have more or less stress and/or freedom. The goals we have in life will be another factor, because the internal "struggle" that one has when it comes to our desires or simply having a normal life implies daily changes and that, in the long run, makes life become very different. The mind always suffers so much if we have nothing to fight for, so it is best to do a little of everything to keep the mind healthy and active. Life is not made just for work, or just for fun; this causes instability and suffering.

Organising your life between duties and desires and finding that balance that works for you will be what will make your life more stable. On the other hand, there are many people who find stability in "no stability", enjoying a flexible life where they do not commit to anyone and simply live in the present moment. Sometimes we have to think about what kind of life we are living and ask ourselves what is the best for us, then adapt to what we want, to what makes us happy.

We need to protect the mind from other factors, such as demotivation and illnesses that can be derived from it, such as depression. These illnesses could destroy the mind and drag us into the wrong lifestyle. Our lifestyle is going to be defined when our mind is healthy, and from there, we can create a life plan. Therefore, being aware of this and taking care of ourselves is key for living.

Without a healthy mind and enough energy, we cannot be strong enough to do our work every day.

Knowing ourselves is important and we must be aware of the problems that we had in the past, those that we have now and those that we may have depending on our experiences, so learning from the past is key to being prepared for the present and future, being a "stable" person and with the ability to handle such situations calmly and without stress. It is part of being more "mature" and growing as a person, which means learning and adapting to things that come, good and bad. The more information about my emotions and how to control them, the better I can look after my mind and its needs.

We must have mental strategies that allow us to have healthy and flexible minds. The first thing is to have a good balance between professional and personal life, working hard, but also relaxing, with moments when we are alone and others with people. We must share moments with people, both on a friendship and professional level, because apart from the fact that it is a necessity as the social human beings that we are, when we talk with others, we open our minds and help each other with ideas, with new thoughts, etc. It is necessary to have a good social life to be happy and feel part of a group of friends, to laugh, go out, travel and enjoy the people you love. Sometimes just a conversation with a person can change your life, and if a person knows about an issue or concern that you have, it can help you with your balance.

However, being alone is also necessary. We must also get away from the noise of people, to be able to think about ourselves, find what we need, listen to ourselves and look in the mirror. When we are alone is when we meet our soul, when we discover if we are really free, if we truly love ourselves, if we like our life… In short, when there is no possibility of lying to ourselves, we can find out if we are truly happy.

Learning to control our emotions and being cold when making decisions is vital as allowing emotions to take over, even for a moment, can cause real problems. As a footballer, focusing on our work and improving is the only thing we have to worry about. In addition, being a footballer, many people will approach us out of interest or because they think they understand what we feel or do; knowing how to distinguish between good and bad advice is something we must learn. Having the peace and maturity to face what is coming, always with strength and temperance, shows the importance of the mind which guides us and supports all that we are, in good and bad times.

Extra comment/thought/feeling:
Luis Soler Mínguez
Sports podiatrist of the Madrid Football Association. Sports Nurse. Former professional football player Real Madrid CF Academy. Former Real Madrid CF Scouter.

From the first training I did as a player at the Real Madrid academy, I received a lot of sports and life advice, to which, at first, as a young man, I did not give importance, but as I get older, I am realizing the wisdom of all those people that we had around us taking care of us; Vicente del Bosque, Laborda, José Luis San Martin, Sr Gea, Molowni, Amancio, Sr Malbo, among others.

The first life lesson that they instilled in me was that no matter how good a football player I was and no matter how good my physical qualities were, if I did not manage to have a mental balance, I could never achieve anything, and this should be applied to other situations such as studies, work, family, friends, etc.

I have tried, both in my sports life and in my personal and work life, to carry this out, and also by reading books by famous writers, and attending conferences and courses which are about mental balance and being happy. But today, I have to be a helper and from my experience over the years, I think there is no better advice than that of the wise men of my time at Real Madrid:

"In the balance is happiness"

But how is balance achieved? And there is the key that another wise man from my family environment, my grandfather Marcelo, gave me many years ago when I was just a teenager:

"Value what you have in each moment and that will always make you happy"

I hope that these life tips that I leave you will help you to be great footballers, but above all, great human beings.

CHAPTER 44

Rumours and Jealousy

As human beings, it is in our nature to be competitive, and therefore, we are also selfish, cold and sometimes bad people. Envy of other people's success is something that happens very often. This brings out the worst in people when what we should focus on is ourselves, and trying to improve. There are people who only focus their lives on envying, passing on rumours and showing jealousy towards others; this then becomes their norm.

We live in a world that is becoming too competitive in terms of jobs, life, enjoyment, etc. There are many people in this life who do not mind lying about others to benefit from their pain. We have to be aware of this, to be in our place and defend what is ours, and without the need to waste time with lies and rumours. At the end of the day, when people talk about you, it's because you are doing a good job, so focus on yourself and try to improve every day in what you are doing, and don't waste your time with fools or nonsense.

The word envy will always be in our lives because when we succeed, there will always be someone who wants to be in our place or who does not like what we have achieved. People will tell you that certain things are impossible to achieve, but because they are the ones who do not have the capacity to make an effort to achieve the goal, they do not even want to try. Therefore, everything is born from people's lack of self-confidence, which should not matter to us and we should not even waste time with it. Focusing on yourself and your life is the best thing to do, as well as having the courage to live an independent and healthy life free and far away from rumours and losers with negative attitudes and selfish behaviour.

Adapt to life, to what happens day by day and from there, always move forward and grow. Overcome adversity and face fears and people who stand in your way with evil intent. Envy is very dangerous and there are people with very little confidence in themselves who want to destroy others, as they are envious that you do have what it takes to be something in life. This should give us the strength to think that we are doing things right because when you are on the right track, you make a lot of people nervous. The reality is that life does not have only one path, and many times, things happen that are not fair. You have to know how to face them and always be clear about who you have in front of you because there will always be envious people and you need to have strategies to avoid problems. Many times, having a good attitude towards everyone but knowing who each one is can be important, allowing you to handle situations, but never go beyond the limits or mix work with personal things; the less you talk and express your thoughts, the better.

As always, we must know how to distinguish between the good and bad people that we have around us, although it will not always be easy. A true friend is the one who rejoices at the same level of your success as his/hers. The same happens at other levels - a person with self-confidence and capacity for work does not need to be envious of others. A real person has confidence in himself/herself to fight for his/her goals and improve without the need to harm others. Healthy envy exists, but it is very different from bad envy. Healthy envy looks at the person with success and learns, using it as a reference, as an example and as motivation to continue growing and learning.

In football, envy is all around and there are many people fighting for a piece of "the cake"; in fact, there are many people in this world who would even sell their mother for a piece of the cake. Not becoming such a person is key, because you don't have to be like that to succeed. Have self-confidence, the ability to improve, humility and intelligence to adapt to contexts or, where appropriate, fight against injustices caused by other people, but always treat it with patience and calm, analyse, act and adapt. Never let emotions provoke emotional reactions that invalidate your speech or compromise your message. Your personality and honour are always above any role or job, so avoid being arrogant or inflexible, but always face it with dignity and courage.

It is frustrating to be a good person, to work hard and to have people around us who are against us, but we have to take everything calmly. The first thing to remember is that no matter how much they want, if you do things well, they cannot take away what is yours, and if they try, you must prevent it. In those situations, it is better to ignore what people say and let your confidence and trust in yourself be the key to going forward and getting to the next level, step by step. Let everyone else say what they want, but the truth is that you will show your happiness just by acting like a normal person and being worried about your own life, not others. We don't have to fight against these people; we just have to be aware of what they are and try not to be like them. Jealousy can kill people, and those people are always the same kind of scared guys, that didn't find the courage to fight for their dreams and need to talk about others because of it. Sometimes, ignoring them is the best thing to do.

The effort that has been made for the reward has its fruits, and success always comes. The more focused you are on your goals, the more likely you are to go one way or another towards the same goal. Of course, you always have to have a limit, and if you come up against undesirable people, bring out your personality to respond face to face, but be smart in using your mind, not verbal or physical force. We have to despise these types of people and not even talk about them. Keep your life alive, be happy and don't worry about what others say if they are not playing with your job or your dignity, and if they are, you must face them.

Extra comment/thought/feeling:
Álvaro Gil Baquero
Club Atlético de Madrid Legal advisor. LLM International Sport Law. Former Spanish Handball Association.

After making the decision to try to dedicate ourselves to this profession, we must be very clear about the pros and cons of the sector. The positive aspects are those already known: passion, being able to innovate, being part of people's lives and thinking, contributing new knowledge, learning and continuous training ... We must also be able to have some cons that are inherent to this activity: competitiveness, misperception of general knowledge about sport ("everyone knows, so they think"), the proliferation of jobs, cronyism, lack of meritocracy, the fight against the "former professional player" ...

This hidden face of the cons of football is rarely visible. So, the mind always tries to guide exceptional or unfortunate situations that we may encounter on our way. But it is convenient to know that these stones were there before the start of the journey, are in the course of it and will be for the duration of our professional career, and that being external to us, we cannot avoid their presence. Another different matter is what we are able to do ourselves to control those factors that can make us doubt the path taken.

Competitiveness is one of the most inherent elements of sports activity since all the subjects that have been involved in it end up being infected by the fact of winning and being better than the other, an effect that reaches into personal life. This shock wave affects everyone who is in our range and especially those with whom we share functions or tasks. Our first thought is - the player who shares a position with another teammate within the team itself, the youth squad who comes up to train, the member of the coaching staff who works with us or the intern or trainee that has just arrived ... assumes a threat to our position, work or job.

Sometimes that supposition is founded, since that "rival" can, with certain acts, make us understand that he/she is better than us, that he/she wants our position or that our work may seem of lesser quality. Sometimes it may be true since in this sector, as in many others, there is this detestable habit of speaking badly of someone and trying to underestimate the work of others. People who use these tactics are often people who do not trust their own work and need to supply their absences or shortcomings in this way.

This is the first external factor that is not within our radius of action. The next factor is that of the highest person in charge, be it boss or director. Depending on the formation of the same, these comments or actions may have one (negative) or another effect (positive). In both cases, our only guarantee is our work and its implementation. If our work is within the parameters and demands that we have imposed on ourselves, the probability that external distorting factors will achieve their objective is less. We must not deny or believe that with an excellent application of knowledge and training, we are safe from any external threat from what we have already commented, but the security in ourselves and in our work will reduce the chances that someone from outside can undermine our work.

The big question is how we can do this. There really is no uniform and general recipe that can cover the assumption, but the necessary ingredients must be kept in mind since they are the compass that marks the direction to follow.

-Self-esteem, self-confidence.

-Continuous learning - there is always something new to learn. Do not settle down and think that everything is done.

-Nobody is essential, so mobility in a profession is a possible and sometimes necessary element.

-Do not do what you do not agree with, or at least express your own opinion in certain cases.

-Do not imitate those behaviours in which we are not reflected.

-Be very clear about the road map, adding to it what we consider appropriate and removing from it what is not.

-Flexibility and putting yourself in the situation of the other person will allow us to see situations from their point of view and will give us the advantage of being able to contribute our vision in this regard.

-Strengthen our winning mentality, remembering the short, medium and long-term objectives and knowing where we are at all times.

-Do not worry about what we cannot control; in this case the personality, comments, and ways of working of those around us, and although they may influence our work, minoritize it in such a way that our essence survives any external effect.

-We should not amplify the value of flattery or the correction of error, since both are necessary for our work to be better and our profile to be improved.

-Always keep in mind that our work is our cover letter, that the paper supports everything (courses, masters, specializations ...) but that in the melee, in the face to face ... is where we must really demonstrate our true profile without attacking the next door, and without focusing on anything other than ourselves.

-Live together with it and know what it is, but without letting its effects undermine or deviate the objective set, to be better and better.

In conclusion and from my point of view, it is important to always keep in mind that there are external factors, such as criticism, baseless devaluation, hurtful comment or malicious interference in our work that will be an element of coexistence from day to day. If we are able to control the impact, with a shield of self-confidence, belief in ourselves and the mind focused exclusively on our work, we will achieve the final objective: to learn, improve and be able to transmit our worth (as long as the recipient is willing to receive it, which is not always the case).

CHAPTER 45

Acceptation and Adaptation

Life takes many turns, so we never know when it will begin or end. It is a path where we believe that we make decisions, but sometimes we are not even aware of why we make them; it is just not perfect. Many times, it is not even fair and we can be the "perfect" person and do all things right, and be a failure, or, on the contrary, be lazy and have amazing success. It all depends on our hard work, the context, and being in the right place at the right time. Knowing where we are and where we want to be is the key to moving forward. Fair or not, it is something that does not depend on us. Dwelling on it could hurt us, so stay calm, walk forward step by step and live our lives with honour and honesty, but always positive and forward-looking, learning from the past, living in the present and accepting what life brings.

Accepting does not mean giving up, but accepting the things that happen and remedying them by adapting, improving and finally winning. This is a constant in life, adapting to the context and winning, without making excuses, because nothing is perfect and problems in life appear without us looking for them; they are part of life. Acceptance does not mean quitting; it means being aware of where we are and calmly planning the steps to climb and keep climbing. Also, to improve things we did wrong, we need to accept our mistakes first and from there, find the best way to improve. One of the hardest things in life is being worried or depressed about a problem we have. It is much better and more intelligent to accept

Acceptation and Adaptation

the situation and try to fix it by adaptation. It is also hard to see how people with good skills and qualities can waste their life due to not having the humility and courage to accept their mistakes because the first step to improving is to accept who we are and the second is to want to change, then, from there, we can adapt to the problem and improve, finally reaching our target.

In order to reach this level of reflection and introspection, we have to accept life as it is, neither good nor bad, only what it is, and more importantly, we need to accept ourselves and our mistakes. We are not perfect and there is nothing wrong with that – it is normal. Each one of us is born in a different context, with different help, things and facilities, but it is up to us to get ahead or not; in the end, it always depends on us. We will never talk about accepting and giving up, but accepting and adapting to circumstances to turn them around, improve and overcome all the adversities that come our way. But first, we have to accept where we come from, what we are and what is happening, not make excuses; excuses are for losers. When we make our own excuses, it is the beginning of the end. We are telling ourselves that we are not going to try and that we have already quit. The way to deal with it is to accept where we come from, the reality of our situation, and be clear about where we want to go, what we want to do, and from there, we have to analyse our options, make a plan to reach our goals, adapt to it and win.

This seems simple, but it is not, because in that plan, not everything that will have to be done will be easy and we will not like everything, but it will be part of the journey on the way to the goal. That is why we "accept" in order to have a solid base, a support from which to move to "adaptation", when we adapt to the environment, to all those good and bad things, but we do it in a positive way. To adapt to the problem and solve it, we must first know that the problem exists, analyse it, generate solutions, implement them, see if the problem has been solved and then improve. It is not easy or difficult; it only requires knowing these steps and wanting to solve the problem.

Adaptation may be possibly the most important characteristic of life, the thing that will make us succeed or fail, and this is because, as we have said, life takes a thousand turns and nothing is ever good or bad, and we must adapt to each context that comes to us. There are many strategies available to achieve this quality. The first thing is to be positive and understand our place in the world. Many people know where they are, but they do not understand why; they do not understand their life and the rest of the world. Having a critical attitude and being open-minded is vital because we need to be critical in order to understand what happens to us and others, and also open to change to be able to improve.

Adapting is key in football as in other things. Do we believe that everything will always be perfect, that everything will come easy or that nothing will ever go wrong?

The reality is that everyone, at some point in their lives, is going to have a problem or a situation that requires changes; it could be a new coach, a new club, a contract, a new country, sports brand or language, etc. That is why we have to know how to adapt to a new context because circumstances change. Sometimes, adaptation requires more or less analysis and work, because each situation is different, but we must be sufficiently aware of reality, be critical and open to improvement, to be able to adapt without any issues or doubts.

Adaptation is therefore the key to success, that characteristic that allows us to mould our character to any situation, and improve even if we think we are not capable, both in relationships with people, work tasks, etc. Adapting means being "unbreakable", having control over ourselves and the environment, and that no one, even if they want to, can get us out of our way, because we have enough mental strategies to win and always come out with a smile and positivity.

Acceptation and Adaptation

There are factors that are key when it comes to turning these words into reality. To accept what happens to us, we must first be humble, and this is a quality that not everyone has or wants to have. We need to have a very high level of self-confidence, because we are accepting failure focused on ourselves, in any area of life, something that also requires courage. For adaptation, we need to have a good dose of humility, self-confidence and courage, but we can add positivity, energy and, above all, an open mind, which will help us to be open to change and personal regeneration. When we adapt to something, we change as human beings; we improve, which is for the better, that is why we must be prepared and open to that change with an open and positive attitude.

In football, as in life, acceptance of your situation is key and your adaptation is even more vital because the life of a footballer changes every week. In football, everything is different and context changes and this will be constant throughout our sports career. Knowing this and being mentally prepared is the key to not failing because not knowing how to accept and adapt to what happens to us will lead to demotivation and failure. It all depends on our minds and how prepared we are. Life is not easy, but not necessarily difficult if we know how to adapt to the circumstances, so to be victorious in the end, we always need alternatives.

Extra comment/thought/feeling:
The good thing about life is that no truth is absolute and nothing and no one is perfect, that's why we can fail and get up as many times as we want; it depends on ourselves.

CHAPTER 46

Just Love

This chapter deals with love for the things that we have in life, most importantly our personal experiences, our family, our partner, football as our passion, and even for our work. It is the most important and the best feeling in life, loving what we are and the life we have, a complete life where we are always going towards a goal and a goal that does not always have to be professional. It can be living a quiet life - it depends on us and what we love to do. When love for something arrives and it is real, it makes you feel intense things, and the good thing is that it comes only with the course of life. No matter how hard we seek it, we cannot push ourselves to love anything.

Everything is moved by sensations, things that come without thinking, without desiring; this is how it works. Many times, people say that they are looking for a type of relationship, or to find a type of sensation, when the reality is that it does not work that way with everything. Real things come or not in the course of life, and there are things that cannot be searched. Life flows and we flow with it; if something has to come, it will come. The human being has become accustomed to always doing and getting what we want and that is not always possible.

What would the human being do without love?

Life would have no meaning without love because it is essential to have such feelings about who you are and what you could be, the people around you, your work and your dreams; these make us feel and feel alive. Without love, none of this is possible and nothing would make sense, because we would stop feeling. Loving and hating go hand in hand because they are the two extremes where love must always win.

Few things give us as much strength and as much desire to live as love, and there are many types of love. The first thing you must love is yourself; it is impossible to love others if we do not love ourselves first. If I love myself, I respect and take care of myself, so I want the best for myself and this is the beginning of everything. Starting from this logic and starting to understand and truly love myself, I can begin to understand and love others and other things as well.

We get up every day, but we never think that today could be our last. We make plans for five years ahead and we do not realize that although planning the future in the medium term is a good thing, we must live in the present. Showing love for life, for yourself and for others is shown by these things, knowing where you are, appreciating what you have and embracing every moment you have. The search for love and spirituality is key in life, so put aside material things and truly live in your mind and in the present. There are many ways to love but the key is to love well, in a healthy way and with the knowledge of what it means to love, what your life means and what you do in the world.

The love for football makes us thrill for it, love it and not give up on the bad things that happen in it because it is easy to live the good moments, but it is in the bad moments that it shows how deeply you love something. Love on the personal level influences the professional, as we cannot separate the individual person from the professional even if we want to. Loving something or someone requires the courage to give everything and sometimes receive nothing, which does a lot of damage and is one of the worst sensations that can be felt. Therefore, the sensations go from the best to the worst, and they are rarely in the middle, in that balance that you always have to look for. We are the ones who must seek our personal balance and seek balance for our life and the things that surround us because love is not perfect, but balance can make it more perfect.

To be able to love, we need a good balance and the mental support to carry on when we are not in a good time in our life. At the same time, we need to take care of ourselves to always preserve our mental health and be able to continue our lives without having the problems of depression, demotivation and, ultimately, events that affect our psychological state. There will be moments when we feel bad, but it is in those moments when we have to be patient, letting the wounds heal and finding the balance again. Love, but have respect for other people or things and for ourselves without doing crazy things and with a plan. The fight between the mind and the heart will always be there, and we must know how to combine both to our benefit.

It is the love for things and people that gives us the strength to be stronger for people. To love someone must be something pure, and as something pure, it should not require comforts or contexts, but well-guided feelings based on a mutual effort to be happy as a couple. Sometimes it is a matter of opinions, but love for someone must be able to fight against everything because it is unique. The person who is looking for anyone, no matter who, is not worth your effort as those people are just looking for company because they don't want to be alone. The important thing is to love a person, that person who makes you happy and makes you feel that you need to be with him/her, no matter if he/she is rich. Real love for someone does not understand interests, but only you and that person together for everything and always. True love is giving without pretending to receive anything in return; that is truly loving something or someone and it is pure.

Love should not be convenient, it does not include social classes, races or countries, it is a global feeling of affection towards someone, it does not imply anything else, no extra interest. Love does not understand what it is to be "selfish", because it is the opposite, it is giving and receiving at the same time but without calculations or measurements. Love does not understand money or comfort, it only understands what we feel for that person; it comes from the soul and is not bought with anything.

Love is a risk because when we love and everything is going well for us, we feel happy, but when it goes wrong, it seems that life is over. Even if we feel that way at first, we have to be patient and know that everything has a beginning and an end. Some endings are horrible and tear us apart, but there is always a cure for everything and we have weapons within us to fight these moments of weakness. Being mentally strong is the key to facing all the good and bad that comes from love.

The purity of our life is marked by us and we are responsible for it; we cannot blame anything or anyone for this. Sometimes we are the ones who go against our happiness, just because we don't follow our desires, and we care more about what people think. We suffer inside because we did something that is not socially accepted or we make decisions that society does not understand; but this is the correct way, to follow our desires and never quit, and that implies love and respect for ourselves and our dreams. You don't have to do crazy things in life, but loving your life means making risky decisions to try to live as you want. The same happens in football - if you really love it, don't waste a single moment on nonsense; analyse the context, make a plan and always go forward to your goal, because if it is real love, you will never lose.

Extra comment/thought/feeling:
Love is everything; what I love is what I feel and what I feel gives me life and makes me the person I am.

CHAPTER 47

Mind vs Heart

Both are part of us, but we require a good balance and knowledge of ourselves to know when to use one or the other. This is key to having control over our actions and not moving on impulses that cause us to make more mistakes than we normally do. We always talk about balance, and it is key because mind and heart represent two extremes that have to be related and be "friends"; we cannot use just one or the other in isolation, because they coexist in us and both are part of who we are and what we represent.

The mind is the one that governs our thoughts, the one that must dominate our actions and decisions, coldly and based on previous analysis, to avoid making mistakes (or at least try) in our decisions. We base everything on control, which is unrealistic but we have to try to have as much control as possible. What we are, the experiences we have had, the context, our security and insecurities, etc., influence us when shaping our capacity for analysis and decision-making in life.

The mind not only serves for making decisions, it is the one that governs our steps on a daily basis, the one that keeps us focused, relaxed or tense about something, but always active in the daily routine. Control is unreal, but at the same time, the more we try, the more we can control than if we left everything to free will. The mind must always be the guide, the one that takes control and supports our path. Sometimes it is cold and does not understand what we feel, but it helps us to stay on course and make decisions based on facts and reasons. We have to listen to it, work on it, improve it and take care of it, because it is the best "friend" we have, the one who makes us be in the present, organizing the future from the reality of the moment.

The heart represents the emotions, the deepest feelings, and everything that comes from within and leads us to do or feel things that we would never feel with the mind. It is, without a doubt, how the human being feels most alive, because it is not possible to explain what it means to love someone, for example, and the happiness that we feel, and it is unthinkable to give a rational explanation of certain sensations or things that happen to us. The heart also provides the power and energy to achieve great things and conquer our targets. The heart can, however, hide the reality of what is happening, so we have to be careful when following it. It happens, for example, when we love someone and everything goes wrong. We don't want to see what is really happening because we are in love. It can happen with people or things and it is impossible to control the feelings, therefore, we put up a wall to keep out the pain.

The heart is therefore very important and makes us experience incredible things with passion and joy and helps us to get energy and motivation to achieve goals, etc. We have talked about love, but there are more things that happen to us in life that produce unimaginable sensations. It is where, without a doubt, the greatest happiness is achieved, and also the greatest unhappiness; both extremes. We must be careful with what the heart feels because it makes us forget what reason tells us and warns us; it blinds us and prevents us from seeing the realities. For this reason, the heart is very good; we need it and we have to encourage it, but we have to know how to control it and not let it control our life, because that could be a fatal mistake.

The heart is an important and basic part of feeling alive and really alive, in this world that is becoming more artificial, programmed and unreal every day, with a lot of background invented by the interests of one or the other. But at the same time, the mind must be the guide, where our decisions are based in a reasoned way, as well as what we do and what we want to do.

Mind or heart, heart or mind?

Why not both? Both are important to our life to the same degree but we have to know how to distinguish which one to use in each situation. From day to day, the mind must command, because we must learn, analyse, be cold in decision-making, and not act on impulse. The heart should appear in those moments when we need more energy, we need a bit extra and it is the heart that, without knowing how, always offers us help and makes us overcome fatigue and problems to regain strength and motivation because that is the heart, the passion for something that gives us the energy to beat everything.

In football, we must let the mind rule because we must control our emotions and what happens to us as much as we can; if we let the heart rule, we will have big problems in our professional and personal life, because the heart, emotions, and impulses cause us to make mistakes for doing what we feel in that moment, instead of using the mind and analysing the next step through patience, analysis and reflection.

We have to let the mind do its job, which is to organize and guide; from there, the heart will take that energy and motivation necessary to achieve the objectives. Everything works and it's useful if we use it at the right time. The heart should be a unique help to give us strength in those moments of demotivation in which we believe that we can no longer continue. It is at that moment when the most intrinsic emotions, memories and feelings appear and help us to believe in ourselves, in having a reason to fight. As footballers, the heart will be of great help for everyday challenges and in stressful situations, where the passion for this sport and the sacrifice are key to our performance. Therefore, although the mind must dominate our lives, the heart is always a fundamental help because it is where the deepest feelings are, and it will enhance our performance exponentially. As always, we have to know when to use what life gives us and keep improving day by day.

To achieve this balance, we need glue and that is "common sense". Common sense means having knowledge and understanding the context, merging with it, adapting to it, letting ourselves be guided by it, "flowing like water" in the world and with people. It requires understanding the world and human beings, not only from the mind but also from the emotions and what we feel.

With common sense, we can manage our life, learning from experiences and having the ability to analyse, learn and empathize with what is happening around us. Having this level of adaptation and understanding of the world is not that difficult; it is not necessary to have five university degrees. We just need our eyes, mind and heart open to the world. It is very important to know ourselves and what surrounds us, as we learn not only from books but also by observing the world and merging with it. Life is learned by being on the street, on a day-to-day basis, in understanding how people behave among themselves, and in how they communicate and create synergies with others.

With common sense, we can do great things in life, because it is a mixture of mind and heart which distinguishes us from animals, using reason, analysis, experiences and all that makes us feel to solve problems or anticipate things that may happen in our lives. It is a unique and united whole that allows us to be part of the world and adapt to it, living the life we desire.

Extra comment/thought/feeling:
We can always give more, and, without a doubt, we can always take one more step; it depends on us.

CHAPTER 48

Freedom

There are many types of freedom and they all correspond to the same thing - being able to do what we feel, what is good for ourselves, and living a life independent of contexts and other interests that are not ours. However, in doing what we want, we must always respect others because freedom and independence require sacrifice – nothing is free in this world; not even important things.

Freedom is the essence of life and the progress that human beings have had, where although nothing is perfect, at least in the first-world countries, we do not live like hundreds of years ago when there were a few who ruled over the others and had control of their lives. It is true that there are still rich and poor people, citizens who do not have options and much inequality in the world, but at least in civilized countries, people can do more or less what they want without having to follow or act as servants of anybody, like kings or masters, as happened before. There is still much to improve in the world because there are many countries that are not lucky enough to have a system of freedoms and rights. Now you have to see what we do with our freedom, once you have it.

What do we do with freedom?

Physical and mental freedom is very exposed today. Since we were young, we have been exposed to commercial advertisements of brands, people trying to sell us thoughts and ideas, and they have made us the products of what "others" want from us. It is good to know what world we live in, to realize and not ignore what is happening around us. Knowledge offers us the possibility of being independent and therefore having freedom. We must try to have that freedom as an individual, with a critical attitude towards the world because freedom is given to us by education and knowledge. However, at the same time, save space and refresh the mind, because it can trap us and lead to disenchantment with the world. All this information that is good to know can sometimes tire us and cause a very serious mental exhaustion, so we have to go step by step in understanding the world and what surrounds and influences us.

In football and as a professional, many things can happen in the newspapers, what people say, our own context, social networks, etc. All this affects us, especially with what really matters, which is our game and our life. In order to have freedom, we first have to want it and it all starts within our minds; if we want freedom, we have to try not to do things that prevent us from having it. Being focused on one's duties and obligations as well as one's life is the key to obtaining freedom, because control over our life is gained by doing our work, and with this, we obtain options, and with the options, we obtain the power to make decisions, and with decisions, we can reach our targets.

You give freedom to yourself if you have the courage to create a balanced life. I know this word 'balance' has been repeated a lot in this book, but it is because of the importance and meaning that this word has, especially when you are beginning to live. Freedom is achieved with confidence, security and inner peace and with a balance between duties and wants, always fulfilling what you must do, but having time for yourself and knowing what you need in order to rest and be happy.

Freedom in football must be earned through work, as it depends on you not having to rely on anyone or anything to succeed - your healthy diet, your studies, your professional and personal relationships, the relationship with your family, your moments of solitude, your moments with friends, your breaks in healthy places and where you feel at peace, etc. In short, your life at work and outside of work. Freedom means always doing what you want but without hurting others, feeling happy and proud of your life, and knowing who you are and where you are going. Getting it depends on you and your context, but above all, on oneself, because everything begins and ends with you.

Freedom is love and depends largely on it. Loving oneself is difficult, but it is the basis to being able to get up in the morning, and, step by step, being able to trust and love others. In order to love yourself, it is necessary to detach yourself from many negative things, for example, the fears and insecurities generated by yourself, and that usually come from the context. We must respect ourselves first in order to begin to respect others and remove the insecurities that bind us. It is not easy to be at peace with oneself, to be free within oneself and to love oneself, assimilating the virtues and defects. Achieving it requires you to be honest, mature enough and above all, have a deep knowledge of your life and what you are; this complicates things even more because we are not objective when we think of ourselves. Admitting what I am, what I do wrong, what I have to improve and having the courage to assimilate it, admit it and want to improve, these are the signs of a winner and that is a truly free person.

Being free is also having the ability to choose our goals because they condition us, but they also open our minds in many ways, allowing us to dream, travel, and have something to get up for every day, which is useful in life. Many problems come from not having targets in life, but there must always be a limit so that goal does not destroy your life completely. Having a balance of everything is the key to surviving in this world full of temptations and desires.

Freedom is nurtured every day. We tend it ourselves in all aspects of our life; in taking care of ourselves, how we work, how we treat people and above all, how we strive to earn that freedom of control over our lives and what we do. Success in life lies in this, doing what we want, and for that, we need to have that freedom, which costs a lot to earn but can be achieved. Freedom is divided into two; the mental side, which is gained through knowledge, self-confidence and all the characteristics previously mentioned, and the physical side, which is earned through working hard to be able to dedicate yourself to what you want, work at what you want and have the life you want. Everything requires a plan, effort and mental health to face it, a spirituality that is only found in the inner peace with no fears, provided by the life that you give to yourself because our life depends on us and just on us.

Success in life is a series of mixed factors that can be summed up to see if your life has really meant something to you and those around you. The rest are all lies and things that people will tell you, because of envy and misgivings about your happiness. We must ask ourselves if we are prepared to accept ourselves as we are, to improve, to be truly happy, to have the courage to be independent, to not have fears and, in the end, to be free. When we free ourselves of our fears, on that day, we will have changed our life completely.

The freedom to build a strong personality with values makes us people of the world, open-minded and with the freedom to do and move based on knowledge and acquired skills. We all have good and bad traits, so we will have to enhance the good and improve the bad, always being aware that we are capable of anything if we really want it. With humility and with the belief in yourself and your abilities, we can get whatever we want, and from there, you must show day by day what you are. This is demonstrated in many aspects of life, not only at work, for example, knowing how to take care of yourself. It is vital and necessary to leave the "nest" and work for yourself to grow as a person, as that's what will give you the freedom.

Life is hard and many people, even the system itself, will be made so that not everyone can succeed and be free. We must rebel against that; we must want to be masters of our destiny and that is achieved through daily effort, acquiring knowledge to have critical thinking ability and not be controlled by anyone. At the end of the day, and although sometimes we do not like it, we have to live within the system, so we must adapt to it. But any system, even football, can be mastered, if "we" want to.

Extra comment/thought/feeling:
Gustavo Muñoz
Businessman and Consultant. Former CEO Giants E-Sports, Business Development Manager Club Atlético de Madrid.

Freedom is not something to aspire to or strive for, but something to be understood. Man/Women not only is but also makes himself/herself; It is the fruit of himself/herself, of his/her free choice, to be who he/she is every day. This natural condition of every person feels different when we become aware that everything that happens to us is the fruit of our own choices.

It is important to emphasize the difference between "negative" and "positive" freedom. As Isaiah Berlin defines it, "negative freedom" is the absence of obstacles in the way of action. This is distinguished from "positive freedom", which refers to the power to make decisions that lead to action and this is how they are established in the Universal Declaration of Human Rights.

Negative freedom is the absence of oppression or servitude and is the result of the combination of the resistance of the individual (or group) and their environment. For example, if a person is in prison, limited by lack of resources or even by the laws of nature, he/she is still free within his/her power and his/her environment to determine his/her being and his/her future although not free to challenge reality.

Understanding this reality and being aware of it is what truly makes us free to walk our way without excuses, but, above all, without fear. Fear is the greatest constraint to freedom because the real obstacle that we impose on ourselves is not facing it and pursuing our dreams and ambitions. Do not fear the future, learn from your mistakes, change when you feel trapped, always reinvent yourself and above all, don't let society, your boss or anyone tell you that you cannot do something, because you already know that it is not true.

When you free yourself from that fear that limits you, that is when you will experience the true freedom of being yourself.

CHAPTER 49

Honour, Honestly and Dignity

This chapter looks at the importance of honour, honesty and dignity in professional and personal life, as the basis of the character and personality of a human being. It has a lot to do with the dilemma between "being" or "appearing" as we saw in a previous chapter. It is very important to have values that are the basis of exemplary and model behaviour, for ourselves and for the others around us, because being old or young, we are always models for others. The problem is that there are concepts that have become old and even out of date because morality has been despised by a society influenced by commercial, economic and political interests; everything has fallen into a pit from which it is very difficult to return. Today, people who live in first-world countries have lost the ability to conform, to feel complete, to be happy with just a few things and with a simple life and this is causing problems and will generate even more in the future because we just want more and more.

We live in a world where, from a young age, we are immersed and influenced by what they tell us, from TV campaigns, brands, movies and marketing with interesting messages from people we do not know and with messages with clear interests in influencing people's thoughts. These messages that are promoted are often about the individual, about appearing instead of being, about looking like a thing rather than living a life based on traditional values. The information that today's children receive is not focused on values, nor on respecting, studying, and leading an honest and dignified life. A lot of movies show youthful characters based on ostentation, rebellion, a lack of studiousness and often delinquency. If we add to this an infinity of adverts that young people see from a young age, we are creating people without critical capacity, without respect for anything, people without goals and with a zero awareness of what effort and having goals in life means. These are young people who, through total ignorance, do not appreciate anything they have and have virtually no capacity for understanding and self-criticism.

We are moved by excessive consumption and always wanting more, and this has made morality become greedy and materialistic by valuing material objects more than good people. This change influences our personality and individual and collective values, because everything influences us, and even more so when we are young. The honour and dignity of the past have been changed for the disrespect for absolutely everything that involves effort and sacrifice. The truth is that parents and the educational system are not in control of children's education anymore; social networks have it and they have a whole campaign of devices and new inventions to sell them messages with hidden interests. If we do not make young people see that knowledge, good values, and being critical are vital things, it will be difficult to change in the future.

How do we build a life based on these concepts?

The education of young people is divided between what they receive from home, and later, what they receive at school, which is where they spend most of the day. Yet now, we have to add the education they receive from TV, social networks, etc. If it was already difficult to instil values before, now, it is even more difficult because it is very tough to control what young people see on social networks or on TV, messages that do not always set a good example. The problem is that, if the young person sees that there are different messages, in the end, they will listen more to the easier, more attractive message, because they are young and do not know how to differentiate between good and bad. This also happens in football. Since they were very young, they have already had mobile phones and profiles on social media accounts, so players are very exposed to messages, criticism or influence from people who should not be in contact with them.

The first thing to do to eradicate a problem is to realize that the problem exists. We must help the people who come behind us, in the academy, for example. Humility is followed by the three values that are mentioned in this chapter, the humility of those who know that the most important thing is who "you really are" and what you show through work every day, not what you "appear" or what the people tell you. We all have the responsibility, as parents, siblings, teammates, friends or teachers, to teach children that the important thing in life begins within ourselves, to know who we are, where we are and where we want to go. All this depends on a single thing, knowledge, and it is something repeated in this book many times. Ignorance is what bad people or bad messages use to attract young people, so it must be fought with knowledge and good values.

Is it hard to get?

Transmitting good values depends on us, on the unique message that we must send from home and school, but also from the football club where we are playing. This book is focused on players who are in that pre-adult age, so you are young, but not so young, and you are old enough to be able and realize what you have around you, notice the kids that you can help, and be a model for them. It depends a lot on the capacity for change at the social level, especially in the way we live; in addition, it depends on education based on merit and effort, not the one we currently have, where students are expected to pass the subject as if it were one more procedure to move into adulthood, not because we truly believe in education.

A person with values must respect others and respect himself/herself with facts and obligations. If you don't respect and love yourself, you can never respect or love others. Hence the first thing we must teach is respect, love and the value of personal effort. Having self-criticism is essential as well; it has happened to all of us that although we are humble, we have had moments of ego or pride that do not reflect who we really are. This is the first step that indicates that we have intelligence, humility, an open mind and the desire to improve, which are the keys to improving as humans.

Is there still hope?

There is always hope that things can improve, but the bad thing is that human beings work by impulse and based on punishments, so hopefully, we do not have to suffer another global crisis in order to appreciate more what we have. Faith begins in us, so if we realize the problem, we can always improve and change, because there are bad examples in society, but also good ones from which we can learn.

Therefore, dignity and honour are not born from within, but are taught and acquired; no one is born taught; adults are responsible for what our children and youth are. Instilling young people with the values that lead them to succeed from calm, humility and daily work is key, in addition to promoting what leads us to the conquest of peace, equality and freedom, the freedom to live happily, respect others and help as we want to be helped in the future. Don't do to others what you don't want for yourself.

The day will come when we must ask ourselves, What do I want to be? What do I want to think about myself in the future? How will other people look at me? etc. The education we have received is essential for this, but we can also improve and enhance our values.

The honour comes from the belief that the "how" is sometimes more important than the goal itself, that the way to get things is very important, as much or more than the goal itself. It's hard to understand if we haven't been taught what it means from a young age. To understand it, we first have to love ourselves and believe in something, rather than living well, having no goals or believing in nothing. Honour makes us a true man/woman, who respects and has the courage to appreciate life and value things, loving the belief that things don't just happen, we have to earn it.

Honesty requires being clear and objective with ourselves. There are many people who live in a lie and they prefer it because it does not hurt them. However, this does not make us grow. Being honest is the only way to look inside ourselves and recognize the good and bad things. To be honest with others, especially with people who love us, we must first be honest with ourselves; this is basic and easy to understand. Have the courage to live a real life, without lies and knowing that we can make mistakes, but with the desire to improve.

Dignity requires self-love and knowing our limits. There are many ways of doing things or getting things done, but when a limit is reached, we must stand up and show respect for ourselves. As with honour, the "how" to do things is very important. The concept we have of ourselves and what we are willing to do to achieve something defines us. If we are able to do low morale things to achieve something, we may reach our goal, but how will we feel about ourselves? That is the question and everyone knows the answer.

These three are concepts that exist, although forgotten in many contexts, and we must promote and teach them to young people. We, as football players, have a responsibility to young people, because they follow in our footsteps and watch what we do to imitate us. It is important not to mix honour and dignity with the ego because the ego is not a characteristic to empower, but the opposite. This is a detrimental characteristic for ourselves and for our lives because the size of a person's drama is equal to the size of his/her ego. The ego takes away our humility and dominates our personality and the way we have to behave with ourselves and others. We have to be flexible and know how to listen to others, teaching young people how to listen. Being flexible and knowing how to adapt to the context are key because nothing that has been said before works if you don't listen. Sometimes having too much honour, honesty and dignity can be bad, so that's why we need a good balance.

We return to concepts that we studied in past chapters, but they are all related. These are flexibility, adaptation and balance. In football, we have to adapt and be flexible, and at the same time, have limits. The important thing is to understand that we are losing values that we must recover and that we need to be more self-critical, think with our mind and not believe everything we hear or see on TV, etc. Without honour, honesty and dignity, there is no present or future for young people. We have to choose, but it is always better to know that we have done the right thing than to achieve things and feel failure deep inside. Perhaps we can lie to others, but we cannot lie to ourselves.

Extra comment/thought/feeling:
Germán Robles
Board Member and Director of Real Sporting Gijón. Former Foundation Director Club Atlético de Madrid. Businessman and University Professor.

Given the difficulties in management, Robert Iger said, "If you spend the day thinking that the sky is collapsing in front of you, you are going to transmit it to your team and everyone around you. This is ruinous for morale and nobody wants to follow a pessimist; it will lead us to have aversion and fear of risk, and we know that if there are no risks, there are never changes". Iger always repeated that we will never have all the data to make decisions, and that is the risk we must take, but always from courage and not from fear, never from fear, and that is what appears in this extraordinary book.

Optimism is doing things well, having total faith in oneself and having confidence in our abilities and those of our team to achieve what we have set out to do. Sometimes people do not dare to set ambitious goals because you spend more time building a theory against the goal than taking the first step and heading toward that goal. With a goal built with good sense and commitment, if we act like this, anything is possible.

It's easy to be optimistic when everyone tells us how wonderful we can be, but what is really difficult is when we are deeply questioned.

Another of the great virtues of leadership is respect. When we negotiate something, we must know that respect with capital letters takes us very far and a lack of respect entails huge costs.

As a leader, we have to be prepared as there is always a risk, and every change when taking risks needs commitment to achieve the objectives, so that personal instinct also plays an important role; if we believe that something does not suit us, we do not do it. We must know that many companies or teams buy not only assets, what the companies and teams buy are also people.

As a leader, you have to stick to your priorities clearly and constantly. We cannot forget that technological innovation will cause changes in management models, so it is about the future, not the past.

In a negotiation, you have to be honest and make it clear what you want from the beginning, and not generate false expectations that cannot be met, because what we erode is trust. We must know that most negotiations are personal, so, if you are in the business of doing things, be in the business of doing great things.

We know that any change produces uncertainty in people, while profound changes produce even greater uncertainty, so become more present, communicate clearly and be optimistic.

When people become omnipotent, they stop listening and learning and this is very dangerous for any leader. We must understand that we are the personification of our group, and by that, we meant that our values, our sense of integrity, our decency, and our honesty, must be the way we behave towards the world, thus will be the values of our team.

Surround yourself with people who do their job well, and who are good people; face your personal and professional life with humility, knowing that success is achieved through effort and also through many other factors that are beyond our reach, such as support, the example of many people around us, or the whim of luck. Let's not lose track of ourselves; keep to your beliefs and know that life is only for the brave.

They say that great stories need great talents and that it is better to renew than to die, therefore, we must never be afraid of the new. We must always renounce mediocrity, get up and apologize for our mistakes and learn from them, be decent people and treat them with fairness and empathy. Learn to live with failure and manage creativity which is more of an art than a science, think big and look for the opportunity for greatness, which is the sum of a lot of little things rather than one huge thing.

Ultimately, life is for the brave.

CHAPTER 50

A Cruel Heart

Even if we don't want to, there are times when emotions and feelings betray us and are stronger than our will. It is up to us to get out of there although it is not easy; it requires self-love and willpower. We have previously talked about the balance between mind and heart and when to use each one, but the reality is that sometimes it is very difficult. When the mind is not right and does not work, we lose our way and we do not know what to do, but when the heart wants something and does not have it, we feel destroyed and it is a horrible feeling, perhaps the worst that can exist. That's why we call it a cruel heart because it acts ruthlessly towards us. It is as if it takes away part of our life and soul.

Where do we get the strength to overcome this feeling?

We must be prepared for what life brings us, and it will not always be good, or even fair, but it is not chosen; it happens and we have to adapt to it. There are many times that we know that a path is not the right one, but we go for it, especially on occasions when we love something or someone and we do it for that thing or person. Controlling feelings is hard, very hard, and even if we want to, there are times when we feel that we cannot live with this anguish, but we need to find the way to keep going.

We must know ourselves well and have strategies that allow us to be patient when facing problems. Patience and keeping control of your emotions, acting coldly in moments of tension and thinking before speaking are key concepts that we must have for daily challenges. We must have maturity when learning to control impulses and what we feel is difficult but important. We have many examples of when we need to be mature at a young age, for example, choosing at the age of seventeen what we want to do for the rest of our life, seventeen being the age when we choose a university career or where to go in our professional life. Maturing is equivalent to controlling, analysing, and having more perspective and patience when living - the sooner we learn it, the better. Nobody likes to be cold, but we have to learn how to be cold sometimes so that misfortunes do not affect us much, because otherwise, we could lose our way quickly due to isolated events, and we cannot let that happen; keeping our balance is key.

There are moments in life when we cannot find our way; the heart wants to go in a different direction from the mind. It is a time when it is difficult to control what to do. We know what we have to do to succeed - be calm, have a good life and what everyone calls "a good lifestyle." But then we make the decision to go after the things we love and we overlook what would provide us with stability; we forget it for a dream, a goal and what our heart desires. Even when we do not want it to, the heart often defeats reason, sometimes for the better and sometimes for the worse. Depending on the situation, we must sometimes let the heart beat the mind, but experience says that the mind must win more often because it is linked to reason and knowledge.

Do we have to follow our heart or not?

Balance is key in life; we already know that. Love for a dream, a person, it's beautiful but hard at the same time, because the best things in life give us a lot of happiness, but also more pain when something bad happens. The love for a profession or a person has the power to lead us to do incredible things, but if we don't have control of what we do, it could end badly. It is a very hard feeling, but as we said, balance is the key to everything.

The tyranny of the heart means exactly this; for example, with the topic of love, we know that we must take one path, but at that moment, someone appears and our life has changed; we are no longer the same person and it is because we are in love; we feel great and could do whatever it takes for that person, but sometimes loving certain people doesn't suit us for whatever reason. It is in these cases that only our mind and willpower can have the ability to find our way and show us what we must do.

Is it a good or a bad feeling?

It's a good feeling in a way, but it could cost us more than we think because, at the end of the day, we have to think and analyse with our minds and not our hearts. These feelings are very difficult to control, and sometimes it is impossible to know how to deal with them. My opinion is that following the heart is one of the most beautiful things in life, but we must be aware that the mind always speaks with facts and is a good advisor, and the heart can sometimes hide the reality behind the feelings.

The heart sometimes rules, but we must know how to balance it with the mind because it is a powerful combination. We must guide ourselves by the rationality of the mind and, at the same time, use the force of the heart, of those impulses that come from the inside that make us have an extra force which is overwhelming and no one or nothing can stop it. Knowing how to use our strengths, and also transform weaknesses into strengths, is the key to success. We talk about getting to know each other and knowing how to get along, which is sometimes complicated even if we are talking about ourselves. Step by step, everything comes out; each person is and reacts differently to what happens in life, so knowing ourselves is essential to being successful in social and professional relationships, as well as knowing how to face the problems and challenges of every day.

When we talk about getting to know each other, we talk about knowing how we react. For example, if my natural way is to react nervously to a problem, the first thing I have to do, once I have heard the problem, is focus, then breathe calmly, take my time, think and from there, calmly respond. It does not matter how long it takes because it is what helps me to react correctly. Surely before this, you have been in situations where you have reacted in a nervous way and without controlling your first impulse. The failure in something must have its subsequent analysis and improvement of that impulsive behaviour; it is the only way to improve and progress as a person.

In football, it is exactly the same; there are problems in the changing room, in a press conference, with penalty shots etc. We have to be prepared for what is going to happen and what we are going to do, so it is also good to use techniques such as "visualization" where before that situation happens, we have already imagined ourselves in it, thousands of times, so it is easier for us to face it. We have to be prepared for any situation, then practise, analyse and improve using humility and intelligence.

Sometimes it is good to let yourself be carried away by circumstances and let your emotions guide your way, but only when they provide us with the strength to achieve great goals. We must know ourselves well enough not to let our hearts control our lives, and know how to balance them. It is easier when we are older, but the earlier we get control over ourselves, the better for our present and future. We should not be worried; life is how it is, and although we are talking about controlling some feelings or emotions that could damage our life, it is impossible to control everything; it is not even good to try it. So, do not be afraid of what happens, but take care of yourself and improve every day as the main thing is to improve within yourself and how you treat others.

Extra comment/thought/feeling:
Sometimes we can't choose what we love, but we can choose to worry too much about things. It is better not to give so much importance to everything as we only live once.

CHAPTER 51

Contempt and Hate

These are two concepts that seem the same but are very different because they cause different things in those who project them. It is not the same to despise something or someone as it is to hate it, because when we despise something, it does not hurt; we just ignore it, but when we hate something, it does affect us personally because we lose energy and time thinking about it, which affects us on a mental and physical level.

Contempt or showing indifference to someone can be somewhat uncomfortable at first, but in the long run, it is good, because we do not feel anything for that person and it "disappears" from our life, so on a psychological level, there is nothing left but indifference and inner peace for what we feel. We are free from resentment or the hatred that would destroy us. Hate projects something negative to ourselves, because it affects us in our lives and we cannot forget it or rest; just thinking about it or seeing that person brings it all back. Hatred destroys human beings and leads to an inner tension which is unhealthy and distracts us from our lives and what really matters. Getting away from hatred is essential to leading a healthy and better life.

Hate adds years to our age and guides us toward self-destruction. It is important not to fall into hatred because the one who hates is the only person who loses something. Contempt is better because we put a wall around the person we despise and we have no relationship or way of receiving anything good or bad from him/her. Hate arises from the need to control everything, and if we cannot control ourselves, it is even more difficult to control others, so we must accept that there are bad people in the world, but how we adapt and how the context can affect us will make the difference. We should live a life in an intelligent and simple way, trying to solve problems out of calm and reflection, not hating, because that is the wall that we put between ourselves and the correct answer.

The important thing about bad experiences is learning from them, not letting them dominate our minds. We must concentrate on ourselves, analysing what we have done right and wrong. From there, learn to live with good and bad people, always staying one step ahead of them. Life is short and we spend much of our time sleeping, so we must select the things that are important to us and not let anything or anyone take time away from us, especially personal time. When we talk about how we feel towards other people, it is easy to distinguish between the people we want in our lives and those we don't. Hating is something that hurts ourselves and nobody else, whereas contempt is simple and takes us away from that inner pain, so it is relatively easy to understand the message we are trying to provide in this chapter.

It does not make much sense to waste time hating when we can learn and enjoy that freedom that being in control gives. Having control of my life means doing what I want when I want and without anyone or anything interfering, mentally or physically, so hatred is not part of my life. However, on certain occasions, we must face people who want to hurt us, and we will have to solve problems quickly and the first time, but hatred is a waste of time. If you have a problem, nip it in the bud and that's it.

To be able to face all kinds of situations, we must have self-confidence, maturity and the ability to bring problems into perspective. When the badness of a person makes us change, it means that they have defeated us and this should not be allowed to happen. Maintaining a courageous attitude in life, knowing who we are and showing it with our actions is the key to a healthy and happy life. We cannot let strange elements produce unnecessary changes in our life. Let's remember a previous chapter where we said that in life, ten percent is what happens and ninety is how we take it. "The best punch is the one that is not given"; contempt is much more effective than fighting, so we must know how to choose the battles in which we fight. Controlling what the context causes us is key to being able to continue on the path that we have prepared since, if everything affects us, we will always have a mental wall that will prevent us from being focused on the important and enjoying the present.

Time heals everything, and it must be added that once we mature and grow, things look very different. Reflecting on the things that happen to us is healthy; it is good for improving and coming out stronger, and it keeps you in a position of necessary humility. We do not think the same at thirty years old as we do at sixty, and neither do we face things in the same way. Being calm and analysing what "we" did wrong is the key because the important thing is the relationship that we have with ourselves. Nobody is perfect, and we cannot think that we have done everything right, so we need to learn to analyse ourselves and know how to bring out the good and the bad, otherwise, improvement will not come.

We are talking about something spiritual, when we feel free and in control of the situation, open-minded and with no fears or worries about what people think. We reach a mental balance when we deal with issues, but without letting them hurt us; that is when we are truly free. We are our own guide and we know where we are going. It is at this very moment that hatred is not part of us or our life; it is simply not there, because we are at peace and confident in ourselves.

When we learn about the things that happen in life and we understand that life is like that, a mixture of good and bad moments, that is when we have enough peace to do what we want without having to share time with people we don't like. We are talking about having the knowledge and the ability to know ourselves, know what we want and be in control of what we want, and not letting anything distract us, which is what feelings such as hatred can cause. Living is not easy, but sometimes we make it more difficult for ourselves and we need to have these strategies, which come from internal knowledge, in order to achieve that balance and know what to invest our time in.

Extra comment/thought/feeling:
In this life, we can learn from everything, good and bad. That is why education is so important because if we teach the good, we will have an amazing future in front of us.

CHAPTER 52

Listen, See and Remain Silent

We only own what we keep silent. However, this does not mean that we do not need to face problems. It means a way of behaving, being patient, hard-working, humble, with the capacity for analysis and above all, for adapting to the environment to be successful.

Having personality is often confused with talking too much and getting into all the discussions and arguments. A person with self-confidence does not need to talk about himself/herself all the time, he/she never needs to speak about others and he/she never needs to show or prove his/her skills. A person with self-confidence is critical of himself/herself first, then criticizes things, but chooses well the "battles" he/she fights, thinks them over and never talks more than is needed.

Listening, seeing and being silent means that we must listen, observe and speak the least because once we speak, everyone knows what we think. It is better to be reserved than to be very talkative as extremes are never good, neither too much nor too little.

Football is a clear example. We are very exposed as professionals, so one bad word said at a bad time and everything we have worked for can be lost. There are many people who think that they cannot change because they are impulsive or very talkative. Of course, that can be changed; it just depends on ourselves. We must know what is going to be good for us and what is not.

Listen, See and Remain Silent

Knowing how to listen is very important because not many people pick up on what others are transmitting to them; they only hear. Concentrate on the environment, know how to analyse it, internalize what people say and how they say it, and recognise the direct and indirect messages. This skill is only obtained from patience, tranquillity and from a position where we are open-minded and really listen to what is relevant, distinguishing between what is not interesting and what is interesting and is important to capture.

Seeing goes hand in hand with listening because we can do both at the same time. However, knowing how to see and analyse the environment at the same time is a skill that takes practice - knowing where we are, thinking and feeling alive, feeling above everything that is happening yet only paying attention to what is interesting, and looking at it with a critical attitude.

Finally, keep silent. Once we have listened and seen, we analyse and, from there, we draw conclusions, so we must ask ourselves what we want others to know about what we think. Is being transparent a good skill? Sometimes yes, but mostly not, for the mere fact that when you keep silent, only you know what you think; the moment you say it, everyone else knows. You are giving others access to the thoughts and analysis that you have done without getting anything in return, so many times, there is the possibility that there are messages that they will use against you.

Therefore, we speak of maintaining an intelligent attitude towards life, not guided by impulses, but by decisions based on reflections, which, in turn, have come from analysing and understanding the environment. It is key to know how to analyse and understand what surrounds us, and we must learn to do it, and for that, we must listen to those who know and have an open attitude and can criticize while retaining humility. Understanding this will allow us to achieve great goals on a professional and personal level.

It is difficult for these messages to reach young people today because we do not have good role models in society. Even in sport, we see attitudes that are not precisely humble, where now the individual prevails, when in fact, teamwork and humility are the most important skills and be taught as priorities. Education has been treated with contempt because that is what interests certain groups of people. They don't want citizens with a critical attitude to criticize the environment; they want citizens to be ignorant. This generates a chain from which it is difficult to get out because positive and negative synergies affect us and those around us. Therefore, we have the responsibility to teach and transmit the good values and knowledge that we have to others, to our friends, and to the people we care about.

Being young is not equivalent to being stupid and useless, and learning to be independent from a young age will make you a better person. Young people often choose between being "cool", being studious, or being an athlete, but why choose? Why not try to "be" and offer the best version of yourself in everything you do? You do not have to choose due to pressure or external factors. Be yourself but cultivate your abilities; read, study, train hard, have friends, go out and enjoy. With good organisation, there is time in life to do everything, always depending on priorities, but there is time to be able to carry out all kinds of activities and actions that bring you new experiences.

Open your eyes and realize that life is more than what you see, and can be more than you think; the world is huge and a life dedicated to a dream, to achieving things, to improving as a person, and to reaching the targets step by step with time and hard work can be very rewarding.

That is why this book has tried to talk about mundane, everyday things, about the reality of life. It has also talked about football, which we love, but which, at the same time, is very complicated and we must know how to progress to keep us in the business. The message is always the same - from a thought, a dream is born, then from there we build a plan, and from there we patiently take steps to achieve it, and it is that path towards the goal that shapes our life. I promise you that this life will have good and bad moments, but it will have meaning and it will bring rewards for someone. That is the triumph of the human being and you, my friends.

That is living and that is life, that when we eventually lie on our death bed, we do not regret anything that we have or have not done. We must get to that moment, and rejoice in life and all the things that we did, that we achieved because that feeling is unique and it will define not what others think, but what we feel about ourselves, which is the most important thing.

Extra comment/thought/feeling:
Listen, See, Remain Silent + THINK, ACT

Final Statement

The reality of life is that nothing is perfect; nothing is as we imagine, but this turns our journey into a beautiful adventure, full of ups and downs, but, at the end of the day, interesting and full of challenges if we know how to live it. The human being has an unattainable desire for perfection but is the most imperfect being of all. No animal in the world has the desire or vital need to improve, compete, or create like a human being. This is a virtue, but it will also be our undoing and we must find the balance in our life.

All of this makes our passage through the world depend on a word, an idea, an attitude, or a desire to do things and we must contribute something to this world and to others. Depending on this and the ability to know our context, we can reach a state of "satisfaction" that ends with death, because we will all die; it is only a question of how and why. Yet how we live is key and depends on us and our passion.

Therefore, and to end this book, we are going to break down some of the most important and outstanding conclusions:

-Love life and live it because you only get one.

-Knowledge is key in life; it is what makes you a human being, and not just that, an independent person, with your own thoughts and truly free.

Final Statement

-Learn to shut up and listen to those who know and will give you good advice.

-Money and material things are important and will provide you with a nice life, but they will not provide you with happiness; they can only help you in the process.

-Happiness is born from within, from the inner peace you have.

-Trust yourself and the people who show you their true love without asking for anything in return; do not trust everybody because they will harm your soul.

-Try to be free in mind and body, think for yourself and do not let yourself be guided by what society and your environment tell you. Having critical thinking will give you power.

-Have a life plan, otherwise, life is meaningless. Create, build, contribute and help yourself and others.

-For important decisions, use the mind and not the heart. Use the heart and its energy to get the targets that your mind set before.

-Free yourself from your fears, as fear is a wall that we create ourselves. Others are not thinking anything bad about you, nor is there anything against you, it is only your own imagination that is cowed. Free yourself and live for it.

-Organization is the key thing in life, as, without organization, everything is chaos and that affects all aspects of your life, mentally and physically.

-Take advantage of the experience to improve and not fall into the same mistakes as in the past.

- "Failure" is simply one more step towards victory and success, so be calm, make a plan and continue fighting.

- "Respect" but do not be stepped on by anyone; have enough personality to be fair with yourself and others.

- Aim to do and not to speak and to be and not to appear.

www.ingramcontent.com/pod-product-compliance
Lightning Source LLC
Chambersburg PA
CBHW020136130526
44590CB00039B/189